Praise ⬛⬛⬛ e *Misfits*

"Brant is smart. Frighten.... just book smart. He cuts through the fat to the soul of the thing time and time again.

"His writing is inventive, hilarious, and always an intriguing challenge to the status quo. We studied his last book, as a band, and it was a healing process for us all."

—Mike Donehey
Tenth Avenue North

"Brant Hansen was made to write this book! I can't stop smiling as I read it and think of the skeptics, strugglers, 'misfits,' and 'outsiders' who will read it and discover that, surprise of surprises, they've actually been insiders all along—as they are, where they are, and right on time with all of their doubts, anxieties, and whatever else that tempts them to believe they are too messed up, too uncertain, or too (insert your flavor of alienation here) to be a 'proper' Christian.

"Jesus said, 'Blessed are those who hunger and thirst for righteousness . . .' presumably because they know they have very little of their own righteousness to fall back on. May that hunger and thirst lead them to this feast and fountain of a book."

—Jason Gray
Recording artist

"This book is one-of-a-kind and such a breath of fresh air!

"If God seems to stir the emotions of everyone on the planet, except you . . . it's not just you! In *Blessed Are the Misfits*, Brant Hansen has signed a clean bill of health for those of us who feel as though our lack of emotional fervor is a disease to be cured!"

—Lisa Barry
Radio host, 98.5 KTIS-Minneapolis/
St. Paul, and Spirit 105.9, Austin, Texas

"This book is for those who feel disconnected, lonely, or spiritually dry. They'd better print a lot of them!

"Brant's writing is honest, quirky, funny, and downright therapeutic. I can think of no one I'd rather have sit down with me and say, 'You know what? It's okay to be you.'"

—Benjamin C. Warf, MD
Professor of neurosurgery,
Harvard Medical School

"I have, for as long as I can remember, dealt with an aching sense of alienation, that everywhere I am I don't quite belong. I am grateful for Brant Hansen's latest book because he helps me see how normal this feeling of abnormality really is and—even better—how far God's love for people just like me actually goes.

"Read this book and feel less alone and much loved."

—Jared C. Wilson
Director of content strategy, Midwestern Seminary
Author of *The Imperfect Disciple*

"This book will disarm you. It will make you laugh and then leave you tearing up with thankfulness. It's that good. This book is remarkably intelligent and thoughtful, but Brant puts on no intellectual airs. He is vulnerable, deep, and deeply funny.

"I'm glad he wrote this. Honestly, I wish someone had written it long ago."

—Dr. Greg Bellig
Chief medical officer, CURE International
Pediatric anesthesiologist, Hershey Medical Center

"*Blessed Are the Misfits* is an EpiPen for those suffocating from the allergens of guilt, condemnation, and the sense of unworthiness."

—Frank Viola
Bestselling author of *God's Favorite Place on Earth* and coauthor of *Jesus Manifesto*

"There are two types of 'Christian' books in this world: Those laden with good, solid theology and dull as a low-res *PBS NewsHour*. Or there are those that keep you reading but include very little depth or theology to sustain you when real life comes a-knocking.

"In *Blessed Are the Misfits*, somehow—like a mixed martial artist—Brant achieves immense readability while providing deep, thoughtful, and theologically sound sustenance.

"It's moving, thought provoking, and personal. It's brilliant. Buy it. Read it. You'll love it. Or you'll hate it, but at least Brant will have your money."

—Dr. Seth Ward
Director of worship and arts,
Central Presbyterian Church, New York City

"*Blessed Are the Misfits* made me laugh out loud *and* think deeply at the same time. More important, though, is how Brant makes us reconsider what 'the blessed life' really is and how it happens. There are many gifts in this book, but the greatest is how Brant tenderly helps us realize we are all misfits, *and* that we are relentlessly loved."

—Michael John Cusick
Author of *Surfing for God*

"*Blessed Are the Misfits* is provocative, and it is also wonderful. Brant makes it clear: for those who want God, He is in it with you. And that's great news for all the 'misfits' who *feel* like God is distant and they just don't belong.

"This book will refresh your weary, good-work-oriented soul. Pick it up and rejoice!"

—Joe Battaglia
Broadcaster, author (*The Politically Incorrect Jesus*
and *Fathers Say!*), and president of
Renaissance Communications

BLESSED ARE THE MISFITS

ALSO BY BRANT HANSEN

Unoffendable

BLESSED ARE THE

GREAT NEWS FOR BELIEVERS
WHO ARE INTROVERTS,
SPIRITUAL STRUGGLERS, OR JUST FEEL
LIKE THEY'RE MISSING SOMETHING

BRANT HANSEN

W PUBLISHING GROUP

AN IMPRINT OF THOMAS NELSON

Published in Nashville, Tennessee, by W Publishing, an imprint of Thomas Nelson.

Thomas Nelson titles may be purchased in bulk for educational, business, fundraising, or sales promotional use. For information, please e-mail SpecialMarkets@ ThomasNelson.com.

ISBN 978-0-7180-9636-6 (eBook)
ISBN 978-0-7180-9631-1 (TP)

Library of Congress Cataloging-in-Publication Data
Library of Congress Control Number: 2017946601

17 18 19 20 21 LSC 10 9 8 7 6 5 4 3 2 1

*Those of us who write do so in
desperate hope that we're not alone.*

—PHILIP YANCEY

Contents

Contents

Foreword

WARNING:

If American church culture makes perfect sense to you and you fit in seamlessly, don't read this.

Seriously, return it immediately, before you spill something on this book and can't get a full refund.

Because this book is for the rest of us.

In fact, it's full of nonstop *good news* for the rest of us: the misfits, oddballs, introverts, and analytical types who throw ourselves at God's mercy, saying, "Yes, I believe . . . but help me in my unbelief."

It's for people like me who've sensed, despite our best efforts and flailing, desperate attempts, that we're "missing something" spiritually. We see others caught up in emotions during worship music or while talking about their warm relationships with God, and we wonder if everyone is faking it, or maybe God just left us behind.

This book is very personal. You may have no idea who I am (and that's okay; people have gotten by for years, quite successfully, without having any idea who I am), but for a little background: I'm a radio host whose show is syndicated across the country on Christian music stations.

I'm also an introvert, a skeptic, and an "Aspie." I was diagnosed with Asperger's, a high-functioning form of autism, several years ago.

On the air I try to be honest about my own struggles, my own doubts, my own lack of emotion in my faith, my own sense that I'm perpetually "spiritually dry."

I talk to believers every day, and I've found there are more of us "misfits" than you might think.

This reality was confirmed for me in the reactions I received to a column I wrote for CNN.com called "Mr. Spock Goes to Church,"[1] which was about my Asperger's and how my analytical personality impacts my relationships with both pop-Christian culture and God Himself. Thousands of comments followed, most of the "That's me too!" variety.

A bit more background: As you read this, you'll see the occasional story about kids in a hospital somewhere on the planet. This is because several years ago I visited a CURE International hospital and fell in love with it and the organization's mission. CURE heals kids with disabilities, kids who are often told they've been cursed by God, and tells them that God actually loves them. That He wants them. That they are precious in His sight.

I now work extensively with CURE, and use my time, money, and radio platform to let people know how Jesus is at work through His people.

Even though I'm surrounded with God-talk—and my own talk—I need to see Jesus in action. Anyone who identifies as a "misfit" can understand the appeal of seeing kids who have been told they are a curse given the truth about how precious they are to God. And then they're healed!

When I get to sit and play or color in a children's ward, I think, *These are my people.* The fact that you picked up this book, and that you're even reading this foreword, makes me suspect you'd fit in with us.

I hope this book is a blessing to you. I hope its message is ultimately freeing, and even if you emerge from reading it thinking, *Wow, that Brant is a very odd person*, you'll also be aware of just how astonishingly *good* God really is.

ONE

It's Not Just You

YOU KNOW THAT FEELING WHEN GOD IS RIGHT there, *thisclose*, and you can just *feel* His loving arms around you, and you can literally *hear* His voice whispering in your ear, telling you how much He loves you?

I don't.

I never have.

Maybe you can relate. Maybe you can't. Or maybe, if you've gotten the impression you're too analytical, too logical, too introverted, too just plain weird, or too whatever for God, you'll let me tell you a quick story.

Once, Jesus went up on a mountainside and sat down with His odd assortment of friends and followers. They were hand-picked, and they weren't even close to being respected religious leaders.

Oh, there were plenty of popular religious big shots to choose from. Respected ones. Learned ones. Charismatic ones. Popular ones. Jesus knew all about them.

He just didn't choose them.

1

That was surely a shock, because everyone thought the successful people were closer to God than others. They were recognized for their insights, their roles in public worship, and their ability to attract followers. Wouldn't Jesus want those kinds of people?

But then Jesus started talking about the way things worked in another reality, an even realer reality, called the kingdom of God, and it was in stark contrast to the way the world operates. Jesus started listing the kinds of people who should be happy that the kingdom is what it is.

And, according to Jesus, guess who should be happy:

The spiritually bankrupt.

People who are grieving.

The humble.

Those who are desperately looking for some justice in the world.

The merciful.

The genuinely pure-hearted.

People who want peace.

Those who suffer for doing the right things.

They should all be happy (or "blessed," in most translations of the Bible) because God's kingdom, the deepest reality, is the kingdom that will last. It's the one that counts.

Not this one. This one is short-lived. This kingdom, this culture, this way humans treat each other, is profoundly messed up.

But you knew that already.

When I was a freshman at the University of Illinois, my roommates were involved in campus ministries. They loved

Intervarsity and Cru (or Campus Crusade) and always talked about it. It was the thing to do.

They were older than me, and they were cool, gregarious, funny, loud, and popular. They thought I was odd, yes, but they had genuine compassion for me. They wanted me to experience their awesome campus ministries. They went to dynamic large group meetings, intimate small groups, superfun dances, and high-impact big campus outreach events!

I wanted friends. I wanted their excitement about God too. They told me I needed to "plug in" to everything. All of it. I would need to square-dance with strangers, "share" in intimate small groups, and go up to people I didn't know on campus and tell them about my faith.

This sounded fantastic to me! . . . Except for the square dances with strangers, the sharing in intimate small groups, and also the part about going up to people I didn't know on campus and telling them about my faith.

When I look back, it dawns on me: of course *they* loved it. They were extroverts, all three of them. I didn't even know what I was at the time (an introvert with Asperger's syndrome), but when I tried doing this stuff, I'd start fantasizing scenarios—say, a sudden UFO invasion—that ended with me being vaporized on the spot.

I longed for that. *Please, Space Aliens, I know what I'm witnessing here is an awesome, powerful ministry and everybody's having a great time. I'm just asking you to vaporize me. Thanks.*

Clearly, something was spiritually wrong with me. The campus Christians were pumped about their faith. They had emotional worship services. I sang, and felt little. They sensed

God's overwhelming presence in prayer, so I'd join prayer groups, dutifully waiting, trying to rein in my wandering mind, asking God to help me feel His presence.

But I couldn't feel anything. Something was amiss with me spiritually, and I knew it. Prayer felt like talking into a walkie-talkie, knowing that the batteries were dead.

Maybe God gave up on me? Maybe I'd sinned too much? Maybe He wasn't there?

Worse, it occurred to me that maybe He had *never* been there. I'd done all the Christian stuff before, including, but not limited to: attending multiple DC Talk concerts, participating in Vacation Bible School programs, repeatedly being prodded to sing a song called "Arky," and engaging in hardcore Christian puppetry.*

But I didn't remember *ever* getting emotional during worship or experiencing powerful prayer.

Not once. Ever.

Growing up, I did remember sermons that scared me about hell or made me feel guilty. So there was that. But that's all I had, after a lifetime of this stuff.

I didn't abandon the idea of God. I didn't hold it against Him, because I figured it had to be my fault. Bottom line: whatever it was I was supposed to be doing, I wasn't doing it right.

---

* I still dabble in Christian puppetry when no one is looking, but that's not the point. You don't need to be reading this footnote. Go back to the text. Thanks.

Then I met a guy named Kurt who was excited about his faith. He told me I needed to experience something different, that I needed the Holy Spirit to show up and *truly* take over my heart. Obviously that freaked me out, but I was willing to visit his group out of lonely desperation.

Maybe God would fix me, and I'd experience the presence of God everyone else was apparently feeling.

We went into a basement in a campus church, and we sat in metal folding chairs, and they shared and emoted about God for an hour. They eventually turned to me and asked me if I was "open to the Spirit," and I told them I sure was, at least I thought I was, or sure wanted to be, or something like that, I don't know, or . . .

They got up and gathered around me and started praying out loud, all of them, all at once, fervently.

They burst out "praying in tongues"—praying in languages I didn't recognize—and I closed my eyes and asked God to please, please help me.

Please don't give up on me.

Please let me have whatever it is everybody else has.

Please. Something.

But nothing was apparently happening. That frustrated some of the rapid-praying people around me. It was chaotic, but they took turns praying out loud near my ear, saying things (in English) like, "God, break through this young man's wall of resistance. Open him up to You," and "Break the chains that are binding this young man to his own intellect and . . ."

"Humble Brant, Lord!"

Yes, humble me. Please, God.

"Help him not to depend on his own understanding! Release Satan's power over him! Do it now!"

Yes. All of that.

"Break through right now!"

Please. I don't want to be this way anymore. Break through, God.

"Let Brant get out of his own mind and turn to You!"

Yes, Lord. Get me out of my mind, like these people.

"Open Brant's heart, God! Do it! Open his heart and mind to You!"

Was I supposed to just start talking in another language? If so, I wanted that. *Kick-start my other-language-speaking, Father. Please.*

Any language but English, Father. I already speak English, so that won't mean as much, and—

"DO IT!"

Nothing.

"OPEN HIS HEART!"

Nothing at all.

After a long time the prayer ended. I had completely failed. I was still "in my own head."

I was eighteen years old, a church-raised repetitive sinner, well aware of my laziness and selfishness and lust and sarcasm. And I couldn't feel God at all.

I wanted God, honestly I did.

Did God, presuming He exists, still want me?

It hurts to remember this. Not so much because it's embarrassing (it is) but because I know this sort of thing has happened to so many people who are reading along. If it wasn't the basement/prayer scenario, it was something like it: a time when we were left wondering if, when it comes to God, we belong on the Island of Misfit Toys, if we belong at all.

God, I don't feel You. I don't get it. I don't understand church people. I'm not having the same experience everyone else seems to be having. I have doubts. I don't think like the others do.

People talk about being "saved from sin," but I'm still sinning. I try and try, but I don't fit. I don't know if I ever have.

Honestly, I often wonder if You're around, but here I am, talking to You. I feel alone.

Please have mercy on me.

If you can relate to that, I'm not alone.

Neither are you.

I was raised in churches as a preacher's kid, and I've long worked in "Christian entertainment." I've seen enough hypocrisy and cartoonish, show-biz religion to give Bill Maher fuel for fifty more *Religulous* documentaries. (A documentary I haven't watched, by the way. No need. I feel like I've already lived it.)

If you were setting out to make someone a harsh skeptic of Christianity, you might want to give him a background like mine. I'll share some very personal things along the way to explain. But this isn't a memoir. It's about how people like me can still believe Jesus is the best news in the history of the world.

As a radio host, I enjoyed regularly talking on-air with the head of the American Humanist Association, Paul Kurtz. He was also in charge of the Center for Skeptical Inquiry and was known for being a "leading American skeptic."

Laughing, he once told me, "You know what? I think you really *are* more skeptical than I am." I felt strangely proud of this. I out-skepticed the Leading Skeptic Guy.

It turns out, I'm so skeptical, I'm skeptical of skeptics. I'm skeptical of myself. And that's led me back to—of all things, of all people—Jesus.

I hope when you're done with this book, you'll see God still loves people like you and me, people who sometimes genuinely don't understand what people are doing or feeling or thinking when it comes to religious stuff.

We have reason to be very relieved.

Happy, even. *Blessed.*

You see, Jesus went up on a mountainside, and He sat down with His odd assortment of followers, and He told them what the kingdom of God was really like, and it didn't look at all like what they expected.

It was way better.

It included *them.*

Together, yet Apart

I JUST SEARCHED "WHAT TO DO WHEN YOU DON'T feel like God is around" on the net and found a handy list.

And by "handy," I mean "awful."

It should be called "Yep, Here's Another 15 Things You're Doing Wrong." Turns out you're not praying enough, not spending enough time in the Bible, not going to church enough—all that stuff. And if you and I *are* doing that stuff, well, here's another twelve things you're probably not doing.

All good stuff, those twenty-seven things. I can't argue against any of those twenty-seven very good things.

They all sounded familiar, too, because I've beaten myself up about all of them on multiple occasions. So the article seemingly comes down to this:

> Q: Dear Expert: Why does God seem absent? Why can't I feel His presence? Why do I yearn for more?
> A: Probably because you blew it.
> Q: I figured. Thanks!
> A: Hey, no prob.

Having lived with this (an absence of feeling God's presence) for my entire life, I'd like to tell you something: *our feelings have nothing to do with whether God loves us or is still involved in our lives.*

> ## Our feelings have nothing to do with whether God loves us or is still involved in our lives.

Nothing.

There is no basis in Scripture for the idea that if God is still involved with you, you'll have good feelings. Unless, that is, your actual god is your good feelings.

It's something few in church culture are willing to admit: "I don't feel God around. I haven't in years." And yet, this is how it is for so many of us.

If God-feelings are gone, is God gone with them? Did He leave us?

We hear the phrase "relationship with God" frequently in Christian circles. But honestly, what might that actually look like? Shouldn't we be utterly content with that relationship?

I know the easy answer is "Of course!" But now I'm not so sure.

We're surrounded in Christian culture with songs and messages that promote the idea that we have found our complete satisfaction in our relationship with God. But what if we're supposed to yearn for something more? *What if an aching dissatisfaction, even frustration, might be evidence of a right relationship with God?*

When Jesus was sharing His Last Supper with His friends, He wasn't just having a Passover meal.

He was proposing.

This sounds bizarre. But there's no mistaking it.

A little background: In their culture, and at that time, marriage happened in stages. There was a betrothal (*erusin*)—which was legally binding—often at least a year before the wedding (*nissuin*). They would not live together during the betrothal period or consummate their marriage.[1] They were "together yet apart."[2]

Through our own modern lenses, the betrothal process might seem odd, but it's intriguing. Here's how it happened:

First, it was common for a father to choose a bride for his son. The bridegroom would then come to the home of the woman his father had chosen.

To her family he would then present an offer: a covenant, an agreement proposing marriage, including a price he was willing to pay to her family for her. The price was an indication of the value he placed on the woman he wanted to marry. (It didn't work the other way. The bride's father didn't have to pay a thing. The cost was borne by the groom and his father.)

If her family accepted, the groom would pour a glass of wine for her.

And now, it was squarely up to her. If she accepted, she would reach for the cup and drink.

The delighted groom would then follow by drinking from the same cup. They would be betrothed. This meant they would be legally bound, and the two had become one. The bridegroom would then tell her that she was "sanctified unto me by . . . the law of Moses and Israel."[3]

But the marriage would not be consummated. Not yet.

Before the groom left he would leave her with gifts, as a way of reminding her that she was bought for a price, now betrothed in a new covenant with him.

He would then go home and tackle his next project: he would build a place for them, a "honeymoon suite," usually in his father's house. No doubt he would think of his beloved the entire time he was building, however many months rolled by in the period of "together, yet apart."

Much as he might yearn for her, he couldn't be married until the construction was ready, and he didn't get to determine that. His father would let him know when it met his specifications.

Only then (it could be a year or two) might the groom hear the words he'd been waiting for: "It's time. Get your bride."

Meanwhile, the bride would be thinking of him. She would be spending her time preparing, along with her friends, for the wedding. She would wear a veil in public, and otherwise signify that she'd accepted a man's offer. I wonder if sometimes, in the interim, she struggled with doubt. Was this really going to work? Had she made the right choice? What about the other options? Had she felt anything for him? Would she ever? Had he even been real? Had she just dreamed him?

Yes, she was fully committed, but understandably eager for the period of "together, yet apart" to finally end.

When the bridegroom's father told him he was ready, he and his party would make their way to the bride's home.

While she would have an idea that his coming was imminent, she and her friends wouldn't know exactly when it would happen.

He would signal his coming with a loud blast of a shofar, a ram's horn, and then he and his party would arrive for the bride and her bridesmaids.

The crowd would then excitedly make their way to the groom's father's house. The couple would go into the newly built honeymoon chamber.

When the groom announced to his groomsmen that the marriage had been consummated, a week-long party would start. Lots of food, lots of dancing, and an abundance of celebration.

It concluded with a massively festive, grand-finale feast with two stars of the show: the groom and his bride. The wedding feast, at last.

And finally they were together, and no longer apart.

On the night He was betrayed, when Jesus was sitting with His followers, He knew this was the last time they would be together.

He gave thanks for the food, and then He told them that the bread and the wine were His body and blood. He was offering a price for them, one reflective of the value He placed on them: His very life.

"This is my body given for you," He told them (Luke 22:19).

He offered them a cup. He told them it was a new covenant between Him and them.

They drank from the cup. They accepted the contract.

Jesus told them He wouldn't drink from the cup again until they were back together in His Father's kingdom.

He told them He was leaving, but He would return.

Peter—being Peter—spoke up and told Him he wanted to go with Him right away. Right now. Jesus told him he couldn't follow right now, but he could later. And He told Peter that he would deny Him repeatedly before that very night was through.

Jesus told him not to let his heart be troubled. And then He said—get this:

> Trust in God, and trust in me. There are many rooms in my
> Father's house; I would not tell you this if it were not true.
> I am going there to prepare a place for you. After I go and
> prepare a place for you, I will come back and take you to be
> with me so that you may be where I am. (John 14:1–3 NCV)

But before He would leave them, He wanted to give them gifts. He told them He would ask the Father to send the "Spirit of Truth" as a helper in the interim. And He would leave them something else, something they'd need more than gold or jewelry.

> I leave you peace; my peace I give you. I do not give it to you
> as the world does. So don't let your hearts be troubled or
> afraid. (John 14:27 NCV)

Don't be troubled. While we're apart, I leave you with the gift of peace until I come to take you with Me.

It's not difficult to understand this as a betrothal. The Bible abounds in this imagery. Even when frustrated with His people, God promised this marriage commitment centuries before Jesus' birth. Just look at this from the book of Hosea:

I will betroth you to Me forever;
Yes, I will betroth you to Me
In righteousness and justice,
In lovingkindness and mercy;
I will betroth you to Me in faithfulness,
And you shall know the LORD. . . .
Then I will say to those who were not My people,
"You are My people!"
And they shall say, "You are my God!" (2:19–20, 23 NKJV)

John the Baptist made it clear that this was the very reason he wanted his own followers to now follow Jesus: they were spoken for. Jesus is the real groom.

You yourselves heard me say, "I am not the Christ, but I am the one sent to prepare the way for him." The bride belongs only to the bridegroom. But the friend who helps the bridegroom stands by and listens to him. He is thrilled that he gets to hear the bridegroom's voice. In the same way, I am really happy. He must become greater, and I must become less important. (John 3:28–30 NCV)

Writing to believers in Ephesus, Paul was unmistakable: marriage itself is a symbol, an image of God's plan for us to be with Him:

"For this reason a man will leave his father and mother and be united to his wife, and the two will become one flesh." This is a profound mystery—but I am talking about Christ and the church. (Eph. 5:31–32)

Paul reminded believers in Corinth to stay away from sexual sin because they had already drunk from the cup; they'd already accepted the proposal:

> You should know that your body is a temple for the Holy
> Spirit who is in you. You have received the Holy Spirit from
> God. So you do not belong to yourselves, because you were
> bought by God for a price. So honor God with your bodies.
> (1 Cor. 6:19–20 NCV)

And then Peter echoed this:

> You were bought, not with something that ruins like gold or
> silver, but with the precious blood of Christ, who was like a
> pure and perfect lamb. (1 Pet. 1:18–19 NCV)

So this is where we are: If you are a believer, and you reach for the cup, you are accepting the proposal. You are waiting.

You are now together with Christ . . . yet apart.

There are those who seem to project that they are completely satisfied in their relationships with God. They seem to ecstatically enjoy God's presence in full and give you the impression this is what a relationship with God should and must look like.

And then there are those of us who very much feel apart. We drink from the cup. We believe He is real; we believe He is coming for us . . . but sometimes we doubt. Sometimes we don't feel anything toward Him. Does He really love us? Given how unfaithful we can be in the waiting, we wonder if it's even possible.

This "apartness" is what, as spiritual misfits, I believe you and I can sense. When we feel something is missing, we're right. When we yearn for more and feel frustrated, we are justified. When we see others seemingly satisfied with the fullness of their relationship with God, telling us we should feel the same, we may rightly feel guarded.

> This "apartness" is what, as spiritual misfits, I believe you and I can sense.

Yet there's Jesus, telling His followers to keep gathering, keep drinking the wine, keep sharing the bread. Keep reminding ourselves we were bought with a price and we accepted the proposal.

We don't need to wallow in guilt. We need to stay faithful. We are waiting, and waiting is hard, but the waiting will end. That's the promise. There's going to be a wedding.

> Then I heard what sounded like a great multitude, like the roar of rushing waters and like loud peals of thunder, shouting:
> "Hallelujah!
> For our Lord God Almighty reigns.
> Let us rejoice and be glad
> and give him glory!
> For the wedding of the Lamb has come,
> and his bride has made herself ready.
> Fine linen, bright and clean,
> was given her to wear." . . .

Then the angel said to me, "Write this: Blessed are those who are invited to the wedding supper of the Lamb!" (Rev. 19:6–9)

And there we'll be, and maybe we'll be looking around at one another, all the other misfits, and wondering how it was we got an invitation, how we got included, how we got in the party.

Maybe it will then dawn on us that we were not only invited, *we're the reason for the party.*

This is *our* feast.

We won't be beating ourselves up for feeling, in the long interim, that we were "missing something," because we *were* missing something. *Of course* we were lonely for God. We knew Him, but not like this, not even close.

There will be no more "together, yet apart." We will be only—and at last—simply *together*, in God's kingdom.

Pretty sure I'll be seated at the misfits' table.

Pretty sure there won't be any non-misfit tables, now that I think about it.

Blessed Are My Fellow People on the Autism Spectrum (and Those Who Can Relate to Us)

WHEN MY WIFE, CAROLYN, FIRST STARTED TELLING me she was convinced I (and my son) had Asperger's syndrome, I was—you know—skeptical.

I don't like personality tests, or any oversimplified (and hey, they're all oversimplified) attempts to cover individuals with categorical blanket statements. (Carolyn tells me I'm squarely an INTP on the Myers-Briggs index. When I deny that I can be reduced to this, she tells me that's exactly what an INTP would say.)

It took a lot of convincing. But after reading and consulting and long discussions with a psychologist I respected, I accepted his Asperger's diagnosis. Now I'm even thankful for it. It explains so much.

Like most Aspies, I don't comprehend "normal" human interactions, like the unwritten "rules" for social cues. I'll also occasionally lapse into overusing "quotes" to illustrate the degree to which all of this is "foreign" to me, like "this."

Take "eye contact" for instance: I hate it. Normal People (neurotypicals, we call them) associate eye contact with listening, so I'll make eye contact to be nice to Normal People. But ironically, when I'm making eye contact with you, I'm not thinking about what you're saying. I'm thinking, *Wow, I hate eye contact.*

Also, people with Asperger's tend to be very blunt. I'm constantly offending people on my radio show and genuinely don't know why.

This brings to mind a recurring conversation I had growing up.

Mom: You shouldn't have said that.
Me: But you told me to be honest.
Mom: Not *that* honest.
Me: Whoops.

The discussions now are roughly similar.

Boss: You shouldn't have said that.
Me: But you told me to be honest.
Boss: Not *that* honest.
Me: Whoops.

Apparently, we radio people are supposed to say honest things but not . . . *that* . . . thing I just said, whatever it was.

I tend to assume other people are honest, too, so I get taken advantage of a lot. I can't tell when someone else is lying or holding back. Why would they do that? That used car salesman tells me this car is worth $12,000. Well, okay then. That's what it must be worth. Here's $12,000.

Another Aspie quality: I don't know how to flirt. I never have known how. It's an utter mystery.

I'd watch people do it and had no idea *why* they would want to do that or what the rules were for it. So I had no one romantically interested in me, as far as I could tell. Once, in college, I had a friend who was a female. She was smart and I really liked her. So one day I just flatly blurted out—because it was true—"I love you."

Silence. Then she said to me—and I'll never forget these golden words:

"Um . . . Thanks?"

We eventually got married. (Suave, no?)

To this day, she'd love more eye contact, I know. I try really hard. I don't know why it's such a struggle. I wish it weren't. But she loves me, and what a relief that is.

She thinks I'm handsome, too, even if my default look is inappropriately intense.

And here's another complication, just to make things fun: I was also born with a neurological condition called nystagmus, which causes my eyes to move rapidly back and forth. In order for me to see straight, I have to move my head to compensate for the eye movement.

So I'm constantly—even as I type this—shaking my head no. The combination of an intense brooding look, lack of eye contact, and head-shaking is not a prescription for easy friend-making.

While I'm minding my own business, people around me think I'm disapproving of them. Even when I'm perfectly happy, thinking about outer space or baby robots or something awesome, people think I'm up to no good, angry, or judging them. Regularly, I have strangers suddenly snap me out of a daydream with, "Well, what's the matter with *you?*"

And this is why I work in radio. I can't be seen. I get to talk, I get to express ideas, but without the concern of the stressful rules and cadence of small talk or offending people with my very countenance. I don't have to worry about misreading the body language of the people around me.

Listeners keep asking, "When are you guys getting a webcam for your studio?" The answer to that is never. Radio is sweet solace.

Same thing goes for writing a book like this. You won't misread my body language and think, *Man, this guy is messed up*. Instead, you'll be able to read my ideas, carefully process them, consider them on their merits, and *then* think, *Man, this guy is messed up*.

So it's much cleaner this way.

Now, many people think that those with Asperger's, which is also often associated with high intelligence, will be less likely to be inclined toward faith. That may be largely true; I don't know. But for me, I believe we have distinct advantages when it comes to seeing how refreshing Jesus is.

Later I'm going to unpack my reasoning why, despite my intense skepticism, I'm still a believer in Jesus. But here are just a few of the wonderful things someone like me finds in being a Jesus-follower:

1. In the Bible, Christians are described as "aliens and strangers."

We have zero problem relating to that. Aspies feel like

we're on the wrong planet to start with. We study neurotypicals, but we do not understand them. There's less temptation to mindlessly assimilate to the larger culture when you realize it makes no sense.

2. *Jesus has little patience for human hierarchies.*

I've noticed many on the autism spectrum don't understand why some people are considered more important than others or, for example, why we should "kiss up" to "superiors" in the workplace.

This can make things difficult in job situations, but I positively love what Jesus said in Matthew 23, right in front of everybody:

> Those Pharisees and teachers of the law love to have the most important seats at feasts and in the synagogues. They love people to greet them with respect in the marketplaces, and they love to have people call them "Teacher."
>
> But you must not be called "Teacher," because you have only one Teacher, and you are all brothers and sisters together. And don't call any person on earth "Father," because you have one Father, who is in heaven. And you should not be called "Master," because you have only one Master, the Christ. Whoever is your servant is the greatest among you. Whoever makes himself great will be made humble. Whoever makes himself humble will be made great. (vv. 6–12 NCV)

HERO.

And He's so clear about this: there are no big shots. Anyone who thinks he's a big shot is about to be humbled.

You may have noticed that humans love to celebrate the same people over and over. But Jesus flips our culture upside down.

Oh, you're a religious talent who used God to guilt people out of their last dollar so you could buy a Lexus . . . ? Brace yourself.

3. Jesus values the underdog.

The upside-down nature of the kingdom is not a one-off thing for Him. He keeps talking about it. The humble are going to be lifted up. The people who are beaten down are going to be shown sweet mercy.

In a culture that regarded everyone from women, Samaritans, and lepers, to public moral failures and children, as being less than fully valuable, Jesus went out of His way to elevate everyone from women, Samaritans, and lepers, to public moral failures and children.

He was drawn to the broken and marginalized. About three-quarters of His miracles recorded in the Bible? Healings.

At the end of His life, He turned to a good-for-nothing guy, a man being executed next to him, a serious criminal who had accomplished nothing . . .

And told him he would be with Him in paradise.

Oh yes. In a world of preening religious hypocrisy, I am drawn to this.

4. Jesus is blunt and gets to the point.

I just like His style. He was stunningly honest, said what He meant, kept it short, and left the learned sputtering.

To read these accounts is to encounter one drop-the-mic moment after another.

He didn't talk much about feelings either. If He ever equated religious emotion with doing God's will, I can't find it.

5. Jesus acknowledges something few else will: moralistic religion doesn't actually work.

Again, since people with Asperger's are prone to skepticism and brutal honesty, this certainly resonates with me. I've seen enough to doubt any claims of my own self-righteous "goodness," and here's Jesus again, blowing apart the idea that anyone can ever be good enough for God.

> If He ever equated religious emotion with doing God's will, I can't find it.

From what I've seen, the world is deeply, profoundly broken (even my atheist friends allow this), and every human I've ever gotten to know turns out to have issues. We're inconsistent, in certain circumstances untrustworthy, and we don't even live up to our own standards, let alone God's.

We all want to think we're morally superior. (It's called "illusory superiority." We think we're smarter than average, more honest than average, and better at driving than most too.[1]) But we're kidding ourselves.

Jesus calls us on it. He doesn't give us yet another "Here's How to Be Morally Awesome" study plan, because He knows we're in way deeper than that. He doesn't give us that because it won't work.

So He gives us Himself.

6. He doesn't coerce anyone. Ever.

As someone who, like a lot of Aspies, has been bullied in some religious settings, this is wonderful. I've noticed that even as we can be justifiably suspicious of human nature in general, we are often naïve about individuals. Because Aspies have trouble reading people, we can find out too late that we were taken advantage of by someone who operates through control.

But Jesus? He lets people walk away. He's sad about it, but He lets them walk. He manipulates no one.

7. He says if you've seen Him, you've seen God.

This sort of claim, out of any human's mouth, is obviously immediately suspect. But Jesus said this in the Gospels many times and in many ways. If I'm to respect His teaching, if I'm to deal honestly with Him, I can't ignore this.

Jesus is exactly what I would hope God would be: a blunt-speaking, underdog-loving, field-leveling, jaw-droppingly brilliant, authority-challenging, short-story-telling, self-sacrificing, bring-the-children-to-Me . . . healer.

And if there's a God, and this is what God is like . . . this is incredibly good news.

Blessed Are Those of Us
Who Apparently Landed
on the Wrong Planet

SO THE FORMULA FOR TEENAGE POPULARITY WAS in place: I had a neurological condition that caused me to shake my head nonstop. I was severely nearsighted and had to have two lockers to house all my large-print books. I had Asperger's syndrome. I was also the president of the Illinois Student Librarian's Association.

That's right: I helped organize annual library-themed conventions, at which we played Dewey Decimal Bingo. I'm not making any of this up.

Just to make it worse, I played the flute in band.

I don't know why I chose to play the flute. But I did, and I wound up being the only male flautist, I'm confident, in central Illinois marching-band history.

Actually, I do know why I chose the flute, but I don't want to admit it. I was in sixth grade and had just seen a *Love*

Boat rerun wherein Julie, the cruise director, played the flute. I thought the flute made a nice sound.

Pretty sure, in light of that admission, if I ever had any shred of "street cred" remaining, it has now been obliterated.

Please know that Assumption, Illinois, is a farming and hunting town. Also: football. That's what teenage guys do. You work on the farm, you hunt, you football, you chew some Skoal. That's it. You do not farm, hunt, football, chew some Skoal, and *play the flute.*

I grew ashamed after I realized I had picked The Apparently Wrongest Possible Instrument. Humans have cultural norms about musical instruments, and while I don't understand them, the flute is clearly not an option for guys in the Midwest of the United States. No one told me.

But it was too late. My mom would not let me quit playing the flute. (Yet another sentence you won't hear Vin Diesel saying.) So I had to figure out a way not to be seen.

I asked the marching-band director to kindly put me in the interior of our formations.

Unfortunately—tragically, even—I was pretty good at playing the flute. I beat out all the high school girls for first chair in the band. You would think they would be impressed by the show of alpha-male awesomeness. They were not.

If you think this is the nadir of the story, that this is rock bottom, let me assure you that it is not. Oh, no, my friend. This is just the setup.

We practiced in a band-shell arrangement, with woodwinds on the lowest level. The floor was a hard tile, the walls concrete block. One afternoon our band director, Mr. Sesko, had us all together, junior highers and high schoolers, to practice for a big concert. The room was silent. Everyone was already warmed up.

Total silence.

A sheet of music fell off my music stand.

It wafted, like a feather, floating behind me and settling on the floor.

I reached back, through the gap in the metal folding chair, contorting my shoulder a bit to reach the music . . . and tipped the chair. It fell over. I lay atop the chair, my arm pinned mercilessly between the folded seat of the chair and the back of the chair.

I couldn't get out. My body's weight pinned my arm inside, and I couldn't get up because my arm was stuck. Please know that a folding chair, under precise conditions, can become a Chinese Flautist Trap.

The room was silent—except for my own lonely clattering cacophony, I mean. My struggle was loud, as it generally is when a boy is vainly flipping about, dying-fish style, clanking a metal folding chair against a hard floor.

No one said a word. Or helped. They just watched in shock and awe.

I flipped and I tugged and I flopped and I clanked.

I remember looking toward the clarinet section, where two girls I had crushes on, Tammy and Jill, watched in a mix of concern and amusement. I remember looking up, as I thrashed about, at Mr. Sesko, still on the podium, baton still frozen in ready position, his mouth agape.

Clankety-flip-clank-argh-clankety.

Eventually—I can't remember how—the chair let me go. I know I got loose, because I'm not currently wearing a folding chair.

I do remember I had to leave for X-rays. I had to wear my arm in a sling at school.

My mom eventually let me quit playing the flute, but it turns out that whatever you were when you were thirteen? In your mind's eye, that's who you are.

So in mine I'm a small kid with glasses, and I'm on a tile floor, in front of a crowd, and I'm wrestling a folding chair.

Sometimes I get to talk to young people who have Asperger's, and it's my favorite thing. Their teacher will tell me that they don't fit in, that they struggle to be accepted by others. I'm sure that's true, but when I look at them, I see the friends I wish I had in my small town.

These kids always ask questions. Lots.

Like, "So why do we have to look at people when we talk? What's the big deal?" Or, "Why do people ask me, 'How's it going?' but they don't really want to know?" Or, "I'm very interested in trains, but people tell me that's weird. Why are cars not weird, but trains are?" Or, "Why am I told to quit asking questions? They say to ask questions, and then they don't want me to ask questions. Why?"

I tell them I don't know. I don't understand this culture. I don't understand the humans that populate this planet, this Earth. They don't make sense to me.

I tell them that I'm actually kind of happy about that. As much as I want to fit in sometimes, I think normal is actually boring.

But I tell them that, because of my faith, I have to love

people. These inexplicable, illogical, bipedal hominids—I have to study their ways. It's not good enough for me to dismiss them and collapse into my own world.

Do I feel more comfortable holing myself up and playing video games versus interacting with people? You bet I do. But I know that's not what I'm supposed to do.

I tell them I've been to many other countries, and all over the world, people have different ways of interacting. I tell them I've always been a very picky eater, but when I'm in someone's home in another country and they've spent a week's salary to prepare a meal for me, well, I'm eating it all. Period.

> I have to love people. These inexplicable, illogical, bipedal hominids—I have to study their ways.

And when I'm here in America, for instance, I force myself to smile. I don't naturally do it. What I like to do is stare at the ground. But I look up and smile—when I remember to—not because I think it makes sense, but because it apparently puts humans at ease.

Why? I don't fully understand. If you already know I like you, why do I have to smile at you intermittently? Whatever—doesn't matter. If I love you, I do things for you.

My wife frequently wants me to tell her what I'm thinking and feeling. This is painful for me. I don't understand why she needs to know these things.

But I try, because I married a human, and I love this human, and this human told me she likes it when I do that.

I've noticed when humans encounter other humans in the United States, they stick out their right hand vertically and perform a clasp maneuver with those hands. Many other cultures do not do this. But I'm embedded here for now and wish to greet them, so I have learned to perform a handclasp with others for this purpose.

So, in sum:

1. Humans make no sense.
2. Love them anyway.

Truth is, we Aspies—and all of us who pride ourselves in our consistent devotion to logic—do things that aren't so logical too. We have yearnings and dreams and desires that can't be reduced to cold efficiency, math, or chemical reactions in the brain. They are things we generally aren't aware of, but they're there. People don't often tell us, I've noticed. We might like to point things out to them, but sometimes they're scared of pointing things out to us.

So, in sum:
1. Humans make no sense.
2. Love them anyway.

This goes for "spiritual misfits" without Asperger's too. Much as we may not understand church culture; much as we may have been burned by it; much as we may rightly reject some of the forms church has taken . . . we have to love people. That means understanding where they are and seeing them in light of God's patience with us.

That is why this book can't merely be a screed against all the idiocy I've encountered in American Christian culture. Somehow God looked at humans, and despite our foolishness, rebellion, ignorance, and self-righteousness . . . decided to live among us.

To love us, He decided to walk like us. Talk like us. Do human being–type things.

And (this is really important to me) He knows what it's like to be misunderstood. No one—not even His closest friends—understood Him. He baffled them to the very end.

They betrayed Him.

And yet He loved them.

It is too easy, then, as someone who's felt rejected, let down, even made fun of by church people, to simply refuse to love them.

It's too easy to live my life in reaction to them. Yes, I can easily craft a false narrative about how awful others are and how much better than them I am, but it excuses me from the hard work of forgiveness and patience.

I know I don't fit in. But I also know I'm supposed to love people, even those who will never, ever understand me and don't even want to.

When I get down on American church culture, I have to remind myself: let's face it, our American culture, as a whole, is absurd.

> I know I don't fit in. But I also know I'm supposed to love people, even those who will never, ever understand me and don't even want to.

We just get used to it. We walk through a mall, and— What's that? A person in a giant bear costume selling phone cases? Of course! Here are some balloons attached to some mattresses. Obviously. Here's a stage in the middle of the mall atrium, and something's about to happen on it, but none of us wants to be around for it, that's for sure. Makes sense.

I walked into a Hollister Store of Clothing once. I guess it makes sense to cool people. I didn't understand some things, so I wrote the Hollister people in an attempt to gain understanding.

Dear Hollister People,

First, a happy New Year to you and yours!

Second, I walked in one of your stores for the first time the other day! I'm pretty sure your clothes are awesome and stuff, but I had a problem:

I couldn't see anything.

I was wondering if I could buy you guys some lights. I bumped into a couple tables.

Anyway, Hollister, I was going to tell you about my college roommate Jeff, who used to have this blind ferret, and it would navigate by always brushing against the perimeter of the room. I was going to tell you about that because I hadn't thought about that ferret for a while. But I thought about that ferret when I was at your store.

Anyway, I felt some clothes in there, but I didn't buy anything. It was too dark.

I tried to guess what the clothes looked like from your advertising pictures. In front of the store, you had a big picture of a guy with no clothes on, so that didn't help that much.

I'm probably not your target demographic. I play the accordion.

Sincerely,

Brant P. Hansen

P.S.—I had this friend, Tom, who earnestly said, "You know, I go to the mall, and they've got the music thumping, and the store people are all cool and stuff, and it's like this awesome party, and then I get home—and it's just a shirt."

P.P.S.—I made this haiku:

> Hollister: need help
> darkness enshrouds your products
> can't see anything

I suspect they had some nice stuff in there. One day I'm going to get one of those miner helmets, the ones with the little lamps, and head on in there and see what I can unearth.

Honestly, I included that little Hollister letter because when I first wrote it, someone shared it on Reddit and it got up-voted a lot. But I also genuinely have a point with this:

those of us who are critical of the oddities of our consumerist religious culture would do well to remember that our larger culture is similarly bizarre, distorted, and misshapen.

Most people don't see it. They've become acculturated. This is their planet. Some can sit through a worship service/concert without a qualm or question or flash of doubt. Some can see an eighty-foot inflatable gorilla outside the appliance store, and instead of thinking, *What an odd world*, they apparently think, *Cool, a gorilla! I guess I'll get me a new refrigerator.*

And then they think we are the weird ones.

So, no, I don't understand this planet. But here we are, and this is the planet Jesus visited. Maybe He visited others—who knows?—but I can't imagine He loved them more.

He knows this world is both cruel and inhospitable to Him and His people. But He told us God "so loves" it anyway.

He even plans to rescue it.

Blessed Are the Unfeeling Faithful

EVERY NOW AND THEN WE'LL ASK LISTENERS ON our radio show, "What if you were trapped on an elevator with Jesus? What if you knew it would be a couple hours before the rescue crew got there? You could talk about anything. What would you ask Him?"

Most people want to ask about pain and suffering and why God allows it. Or they want to know how their grandma's doing. That kind of thing.

Fair enough, but I know what I would want to ask Him.

If I could choke out the question, I'd want to ask this:

Am I a fraud?

Please tell me I'm not. Please tell me You're proud of me. Please tell me You know I struggle, but no, I'm not a fraud at all. I'd love to hear it.

I know, in my head, all about grace, and I'm so thankful for it. I think it's beautiful. I know, in my head, that God loves sinners and failures. But I feel like everything I do is tainted with some selfishness. And with my seeming inability to sense God's presence . . . is it possible God could still be proud of me?

———————

Oddly enough, this fraud issue comes to mind, for some, with regard to Teresa of Calcutta, now a Catholic saint, after her correspondence of nearly fifty years was made public.

Here she was, an outspoken follower of Jesus on an international stage, but when it came to warm, religious feelings, she had nothing. And that bothered her deeply. She kept serving the poor, kept praying, kept leading, but she confided in her letters to confessors that she also felt like God had abandoned her.

She wrote that "the silence and emptiness is so great that I look and do not see, listen and do not hear."[1]

Just a few months later she was onstage in Oslo, accepting the Nobel Peace Prize, talking confidently of a Jesus she knew, a Christ who brings joy for all of us.

When she started her mission in Calcutta in the 1940s, she was young and excited and felt so close to God. Then, from 1948 until her death in 1997, she was spiritually dry. Yet she continued as an outspoken missionary.

Was she a fake?

Christopher Hitchens certainly thought so. The late, leading atheist and tremendously gifted writer wrote a book accusing Teresa of running from the obvious: her lack of God-feelings were due to the fact that God didn't exist. He said, "She was no more exempt from the realization that religion is a human fabrication than any other person . . ."[2]

If she was a fake, I'm not even sure what that makes me. She sacrificed her own comfort to care for the sick and dying.

Me? I get paid to talk between the songs on the radio.

I subtitled this book *Great News for Believers Who Are Introverts, Spiritual Strugglers, or Just Feel Like They're Missing Something*, and I really mean it.

Those of us who don't get much, or any, emotional reward from our spiritual lives are in such great company. I'm convinced there are far more of us than are willing to admit to it. Perhaps we fear less what others might think of us than what it might mean to hear ourselves say the words: *If the feeling is gone, maybe this whole thing is a charade.*

> **Those of us who don't get much, or any, emotional reward from our spiritual lives are in such great company.**

Psychiatrist and theologian Gerald May wrote about this sense of loss in his book *The Dark Night of the Soul*:

> It is easy to understand how devastating such an experience might be. For people who are deeply in love with God, the loss of a habitual sense of God's presence can seem like a

greater abandonment than the loss of human love. Here again, people are likely to feel it is somehow their fault; they wonder where they went so wrong to cause the divine Lover to disappear. And when this loss is accompanied by lassitude and emptiness in prayer and other spiritual practices and lack of motivation for them, a person may easily wonder, "Do I even believe in anything anymore? Do I even care?"[3]

The good news, according to May, is that the "dark night" is actually a wonderful thing. He wrote that it's ultimately liberating. We become less dependent on our feelings. Even the "dark" part of the dark night isn't to be feared; it's only dark in the sense that *hidden* things are happening.

Mysterious things, yes, but good things: We're growing up. We become less self-focused. Our faith becomes less about the comings and goings of emotion and more about loving people freely.

Sure, a lot of people have a very visceral sense of God's presence. But if you talk to them about it, and I have, you find that this sense can be a bit lopsided.

For instance, many people I've talked to say they have an emotive sense of God's presence as an all-accepting, warm-hugging, positive, permission-granting, affirming friend. Others feel Him as a perpetual rebuker; an all-watching ogre, ready to judge and punish every failure or sinful, immature thought. There's a lot of psychology going on here.

In any case, let's acknowledge that all of our impressions of God are incomplete, and they're only that: impressions.

If I mistake my impression, or my feelings, for the real God, I'm committing idolatry.

If I mistake God's gifts, however profound, experiential, or soothing, for God Himself, I'm committing idolatry.

In Scripture He clearly didn't want His people worshipping a mere impression of Him. Not because He is distant and unknowable, but because He is ever close. We don't need to worship images if we have the Real Thing.

And the Real Thing does not promise a weekly sensory experience of His presence. Biblically, there's no basis for expecting such a thing.

Nor is there reason to *expect* to "hear God's audible voice" on anything like a regular basis, or even at all. I love how Adam McHugh described how God might speak to introverts, in particular:

> God's speech to introverts may come in the form of inward
> thoughts or impulses, ideas that spring out at us, or words,
> images, or feelings that surprise us or cut against the grain
> of our natural tendencies.[4]

There's nothing terribly spectacular-seeming about that. But if I actually *do* something that cuts against the grain of my natural tendency, well, that sounds like obedience, which God apparently regards as pretty spectacular, indeed.

Yes, we read in the Bible where God communicates through a burning bush here and a prophet there. But it's nothing like what we might expect if we were only to listen to writers/teachers/friends who claim to hear God's audible voice regularly.

Imagine if Noah wrote a book: *How to Get God to Speak to You Five Times over 950 Years.*

In Genesis, we get Abraham going decades without God's

audible voice. Isaac apparently heard it twice in his lifetime. Rebekah? Once.

There are about four hundred years of apparent "silence" from God between the Old and New Testaments.

In the New Testament book of Acts, God clearly communicates with people in different ways, but once again there is little of "God's audible voice." In fact, the only place I can find it is in Paul's conversion on the road to Damascus.

We see incidents where we might have expected God's audible voice to roar, or at least a dramatic entrance from an angel with a proclamation. Instead, we get Peter trying to determine God's will by "casting lots" (essentially, rolling dice) in Acts 1. The apostles had to choose men to take care of widows in Acts 6, but again, there's no obvious voice. In Acts 15, there's a major dispute, a crisis over doctrine, and they don't get an obvious, miraculous word from heaven. They just have to work it out.

So you've never heard God, out loud, speaking to you? That can be alarming for a believer. But it is not unreasonable to believe that someone God loves, someone He's pleased with, could go his or her whole life without hearing God speak out loud.

In fact, it seems the norm. Clearly, God could speak to me right now, out loud, if He wanted to, and maybe He will by the time I'm finished with this paragraph. He can do what He wants, when He wants. But it's simply not fair to create an expectation among people that God *will* speak to them in this way.

In talking with friends about this, believers who seem to have grown in patience, kindness, love, joy, gentleness—the fruit of the Spirit—I find a far more common, less spectacular experience: sudden ideas, seemingly out of nowhere, that prompt us to do something we normally wouldn't. Like things that involve self-sacrifice or going out of our comfort zones. Things others aren't normally willing to do. Small things. Things that are consonant with what we see in Scripture about Jesus. Selfless things.

Might some people refer to that experience as "God's audible voice"? Some do, but they shouldn't, because life is confusing enough.

You can go to a picture-perfect, deserted beach at sunrise with your Bible and your coffee. You can try to clear your head of all distractions. You can pray expectantly. You can wait and listen. But if you don't hear an audible voice, it doesn't mean He doesn't exist, or that He doesn't love you. I fully realize I used a quadruple-negative in that last sentence, and I'm actually kind of proud of it, but I think you can follow me.

It's simply not fair to create an expectation for a certain kind of emotion, intimacy, or experience with God that is, frankly, more the exception than the rule.

As far as I can tell, God does not speak audibly to most Christians. T. M. Luhrmann, a psychological anthropologist at Stanford, studied this very issue among self-describing evangelicals. She found that only about one in ten claim to have heard God's voice audibly.[5]

The point here isn't to suggest those individuals who've heard from God in this way are crazy, or that they're imagining things. It's merely to say that it's not something we should expect while we're still "together, yet apart." If we do, we may be misled into thinking that we're somehow less, or that God loves us less than He does.

So much Christian pop/worship music raises the level of experiential expectation too. While some can easily sing along with, "Jesus, I can feel Your love around me," others don't quite understand. The songs often go something like this:

Hold me, God, oh, hold me
I just want to hear You whisper, "I love you"
You're the one for me
There's nothing like the feeling of Your arms
*   around me*

You may have no problems singing this. (I feel like we might as well be singing "You're the One That I Want" from *Grease*.) It's just baffling for some of us, and that doesn't mean we are less spiritual, less mature, or less loved by God.

It's taken me many years to accept that my lack of emotional response to this sort of lyric isn't indicative of God's absence from my life.

It's no wonder so many analytical types find themselves estranged from a Christian subculture that traffics in emotional appeals. We find ourselves wondering what's wrong with us, perhaps even begging God to make Himself real to us in the way He clearly is to others.

When we're told we're "not open to the Spirit" or "leaning too much on our intellect," we may redouble our efforts to somehow fix what's wrong with us, before finally drifting away.

Someone might wonder where we went. Someone else might answer, "You know, they always did seem kind of odd."

Now, back to Mother Teresa:

> It's no wonder so many analytical types find themselves estranged from a Christian subculture that traffics in emotional appeals.

"The tendency in our spiritual life but also in our more general attitude toward love is that our feelings are all that is going on," [Rev. Brian Kolodiejchuk] says. "And so to us the totality of love is what we feel. But to really love someone requires commitment, fidelity and vulnerability. Mother Teresa wasn't 'feeling' Christ's love, and she could have shut down. But she was up at 4:30 every morning for Jesus, and still writing to him . . ."[6]

There's really something beautiful about serving, about faithfulness, without an obvious, immediate, emotional reward.

It's funny; as I was typing that last paragraph, my wife brought me some hot tea. Now, you should know she's a brilliant, accomplished woman, and we're not newlyweds. We've been married for twenty-seven years. Perhaps she feels "in love" with me right now, perhaps she's flooded with good feelings toward me at this precise moment, but I doubt it.

It's not that she shouldn't have those wonderful feelings; of course she should be in complete infatuation watching me hover over this laptop, repeatedly typing sentences and then deleting them. But we've been married long enough that I know her kindness toward me isn't dependent on it.

There may be, at this time in her, no warm feelings toward me, but that kindness, that servanthood, is an expression of real love. It's not an inferior love, or a sad, dutiful replacement-love for romantic infatuation either.

It's profound. It's life giving. It's sustaining. Feelings come and go and prompt many songs, but servant-love is purer poetry.

Please know that *this* is the kind of love God is seeking. It's not a hidden theme of Scripture.

The absence of feeling is not the absence of love. Yes, you may occasionally feel things, maybe even intensely, but when those feelings vacillate, it doesn't mean you love God less.

He doesn't seem to prioritize emotion. He's looking for obedience. For faithfulness. For mercy. For justice. For compassion on the poor.

Look what He said through the prophet Amos:

> Justice is a lost cause. Evil is epidemic.
> Decent people throw up their hands.
> Protest and rebuke are useless,
> a waste of breath.
>
> Seek good and not evil—
> and live!
> You talk about GOD, the God-of-the-Angel-Armies,
> being your best friend.
> Well, *live* like it,
> and maybe it will happen. . . .

"I can't stand your religious meetings.

I'm fed up with your conferences and conventions.

I want nothing to do with your religion projects,

your pretentious slogans and goals.

I'm sick of your fund-raising schemes,

your public relations and image making.

I've had all I can take of your noisy ego-music.

When was the last time you sang to *me?*

Do you know what I want?

I want justice—oceans of it.

I want fairness—rivers of it.

That's what I want. That's *all* I want." (Amos 5:13–14, 21–24 THE MESSAGE)

That's blunt. I love it.

It turns out that even we, the emotionally robotic, can give God what He really wants.

Sure, I may not have the same "worship experience" as the rest of the crowd at a musical event, but I can offer God the worship He *really* desires: Mercy. Fairness. Justice.

I may have never heard God's voice audibly, but I can still obey.

My whole life may tend toward apparent spiritual dryness. But I can still love God and my neighbor.

> **It turns out that even we, the emotionally robotic, can give God what He really wants.**

So here's a question for you:

Let's say you're like Mother Teresa (or me, for that matter) and you don't feel God's presence often, if at all. What if, somehow, you knew that this would *always* be the case, for the rest of your life? What if you knew you'd never get the warm feelings others get, you'd never have your desire for a sense of God's closeness fulfilled, during this lifetime? What if you knew it would always be this way, until you die?

What would it change?

Wesley Hill wrote of the "fated warrior" idea found in Norse and Teutonic lore. This heroic warrior heads into battle, knowing he will lose, but also knowing he's doing the right thing.

> Since making this discovery, I have thought often that this ide-alized picture resonates profoundly with the Christian story. One of the hardest-to-swallow, most countercultural, counter-intuitive implications of the gospel is that bearing up under a difficult burden with patient perseverance is a good thing. The gospel actually advocates this kind of endurance as a daily "dying" for and with Jesus. While those in the grip of Christ's love will never experience *ultimate* defeat, there is a profound sense in which we must face our struggles now knowing there may be no real relief this side of God's new creation. We may wrestle with a particular weakness all our lives. But the call remains: *Go into battle.* "There is much virtue in bearing up under a long, hard struggle," a friend of mine once told me, even if there is no apparent "victory" in the short run.[7]

Yes, you and I may long for a connection with God that's palpable and undeniably certain. We may want to feel the "warmth of His embrace" on demand. We may want all of our nagging questions answered.

But the Bible certainly tempers expectations for this.

In time, we'll experience Him in full. There will be an end to your dark night of the soul. But . . . not yet.

Now we see things imperfectly, like puzzling reflections in a mirror, but then we will see everything with perfect clarity. All that I know now is partial and incomplete, but then I will know everything completely, just as God now knows me completely. (1 Cor. 13:12 NLT)

For now, as Hill wrote, the call remains: "*Go into battle.*"

SIX

Blessed Are the Unfeeling Faithful, Part 2: Real "Fruit"

IF YOU CAN'T RELY ON YOUR FEELINGS, HOW CAN you tell God is *there*, working in your life?

Jesus said if you want to judge a tree, you look at its fruit.

Someone might immediately, like clockwork, break down in tears of genuine emotion at the first chord of every worship song. Wonderful. But that's not "fruit," biblically speaking.

A Christianity that's one-emotional-size-fits-all simply isn't fair. You may have Asperger's, like I do. You may have gone through trauma as a kid. You might grapple with depression and just not emote like other people. You may be wired differently.

When one person insinuates that another must be spiritually lacking because of a dearth of feeling, it's worthwhile pointing out this is utterly foreign to the biblical concept of bearing fruit.

Here's some stuff Jesus didn't say:

"Does the tree have amazing spiritual experiences? If yes, it's a good tree, right there. Yep."

"Want to know what kind of tree you're dealing with? Just ask the tree. If it offers powerful-sounding prayer, you can trust it."

"You know what kind of tree you're dealing with if the tree leads an awesome ministry. If it does that, it must be an awesome ministry tree."

"If the tree is kind of a big deal, if it sings great and has a Christian record deal, it's legit. Take it to the bank."

Nope. He said you look at the fruit. That's what falls out of the tree when you bump into it.

Of course, we're talking about people here. What's "fruit," then? Not a Christian vocabulary. Not the position a person occupies in church culture. Even "ministry impact" is not fruit. (There've been many who've reached thousands for Christ who've been found out as utter frauds. In the Old Testament, God once spoke through a jackass, and yes, He's still doing it.)

Paul wrote in Galatians 5:22–23 that "fruit" from God is this stuff: *love, joy, peace, patience, kindness, goodness, faithfulness, gentleness, and self-control.*

So if you happen to bump into a tree—or shake it, bother it, or threaten it—see what falls. Was it love? Gentleness? Or something else?

A woman in South Carolina saw her unarmed son hunted down by a policeman and shot to death. Her boy had done nothing wrong. She tearfully told TV reporters she had no choice, because of what God had done for her: she would have to forgive.

Wow.

Bump into a tree, and see what falls. Sometimes it's love and gentleness. Now you see what kind of tree it is.

A high-profile preacher had an associate whose speaking style was popular. The associate was a threat to the preacher's attention and status. His reaction? He forced the associate out.

Bump into a tree, and see what falls. Sometimes it's jealousy, anger, and power plays. Now you see what kind of tree it is.

Jesus was betrayed, abandoned, and publicly humiliated, and while His life was being ripped from Him, He prayed for forgiveness for the very people who were killing Him. He intervened to defend them.

Bump into a tree, and see what falls. Sometimes it's love and self-control. Now you see what kind of tree it is.

A bizarre personal story: I was told by a CEO of a high-profile Christian ministry that I'd slandered him on Facebook. I'd personally attacked him, he said, saying misleading and personal things. Sure, I might think it's just social media, or I have a First Amendment right, but his lawyer told him he had a great case against me. And, he told me, he'd used his lawyer before to "crush" people, and now this was a legal matter.

I formulated a brilliant legal response, which I'll quote here verbatim: "Uh . . . what?"

I had no idea what he was talking about.

As he now knows, I hadn't written a single word about him. He'd been lied to by another ministry leader in the organization.

He's decades older than I am and, one would hope, a mature believer. But when his reputation was seemingly threatened, he decided to attempt to intimidate. Never mind the scriptural prohibition against suing a Christian brother, the lack of evidence, or the fact that such a thing would be profoundly out of character for what he knows of me.

Bump into a tree, and see what falls. Sometimes it's lawyers. Now you see what kind of tree it is.

Years ago I had a boss who loved my work. But the time came when I needed to make a move for my family, which I explained to him, and then left for a "competitor." In his mind it was a major blow for his company. He told me he understood, but he was hurt. His reaction?

He blessed me. And in the years following, he wrote me encouraging e-mails, telling me how much my show still meant to his family—they were still listening!—and what God was teaching them through me. I'd left, but his encouragement kept going.

Bump into a tree, and see what falls. Sometimes it's patience and kindness. Now you see what kind of tree it is.

God help me, and help us all. It's easy to feign spirituality in a culture that still offers worldly rewards for it. It's easy, too, to redefine "fruit" to fit our positive feelings or religious résumés instead of, you know, actually being patient and kind.

But when someone bumps against us, when they zap us on Facebook, threaten us, throw us under the bus, or cut in front of us in line at CVS . . . see what falls. Here's hoping it isn't toxic.

Let's hope it's the real, life-giving stuff.

I'm happy for people who get warm spiritual feelings. Genuinely. I bet that's a wonderful thing.

But feelings aren't trustworthy. They're dependent on too many things, including what I ate today, whether I got a nap, if there are clouds in the sky, or how much coffee I just had. God's love for me, on the other hand, does not depend on what I ate today, whether I got a nap, if there are clouds in the sky, or how much coffee I just had.

"Repentance is not an emotion," wrote Eugene Peterson. "It is not feeling sorry for your sins. It is a decision."[1]

Emotions are very human. But faithfulness, in spite of emotion, and in the absence of emotion, is beautiful.

Faithfulness is a real fruit of the Spirit. And when we get to see it in action, it's breathtaking, at least to me. While church worship services don't make me particularly emotional, here's what does: operating room worship services.

Traveling to CURE hospitals, I see little kids just lying there asleep under a bright light, so tiny on a table, and I see the surgeons and techs gathered around, praying for the child before they begin their work . . . I often have to leave the OR to collect myself. As I watch them work, with their steady hands, I think about the years of faithfulness in their own study and practice. I think about their commitment to serve these little outcasts.

And these children are really, truly outcasts. They've been cast out. In the world's economy, they are just scraps of life. The kids who arrive at CURE's doors are thought of as irrelevant. In some cases, they haven't even been named.

Because they have a disability, they're often last to eat in their own families—if there's food left at all. They often aren't allowed to go to school. They're left behind, in the dark, unsupervised, utterly vulnerable to all kinds of abuse.

Oftentimes, when they're born with an apparent disability,

their fathers leave the family. They don't want to be stuck with a "cursed" child. In many cases, villages force moms to leave the area, for fear the curse will be borne by the entire community. People run away from them.

Their babies are called freaks. Monsters.

Cursed. Friendless. Penniless. Rejected. Abused. Abandoned. Unprotected. Monsters.

But imagine this: when a mom walks in a CURE hospital in desperate hope someone can help, the staff is trained to greet her at the door and tell her something she's likely never, ever heard before, not once:

"Your baby is beautiful!"

"Can I hold her?"

I'm not telling you about this to tell you about CURE, although if you want to get involved, that's great. I'm telling you that I'm drawn to this expression of Christianity. I can't stay away from it.

I live in a culture that makes no sense to me. I'm also ensconced in a church culture that seldom makes sense to me.

But this? *This makes sense to me.*

This looks like Jesus.

Seeing little bodies prayed over and knit back together, by loving, competent, healing hands . . . this looks right.

So, yes, apparently I *do* get emotional. I may be an alien. I may be on the outside looking in. I may have seen horrible things associated with Christianity. I may not understand the American Christian subculture, or fit into it. I may feel like a stranger. But every once in a while, I see something that makes sense, and I can actually, finally *feel* it.

I think it happens when I get a glimpse of home.

Blessed Are the Introverted Evangelical Failures

SOME PEOPLE THINK DOING PEOPLE-STUFF IS EASY.

These are the Normal People. If you are a Normal Person, I appreciate and admire you. I'm thankful for you. I mean, I don't *understand* you, Normal Person, but I love you.

I've also tried to be you. This did not work.

When I was nineteen, I took a job at a shoe store because I wanted to learn how to interact with humans, and humans, I noticed, wear shoes, and are attracted to places where shoes are displayed. This is called The Mall.

I also wanted to wear a referee shirt in one of those places.

Ergo: Foot Locker.

The shoe guys wearing ref shirts were pretty cool, so I was nervous to interview and knew my people skills weren't great, but I landed the job! I was assigned on the first day to the back room to organize shoeboxes. It was like a big game of ShoeTetris, and I liked that, but still looked forward to the next

day when they would give me my ref shirt and make me a salesman out in public, underneath the big fake scoreboard-thing.

They needed me to "learn the system" first, so I did that.

The next day they needed me in the back room again, so I
did that again. I would have to wait another day, the manager
told me. He was a nice guy. He ordered a ref shirt for me and
said he would have it tomorrow.

The next day I was put in the back room by myself with
the shoeboxes, and I organized them. I awaited my referee
shirt and the chance to interact with humans.

For my next shift, they had me organize shoeboxes in the
back room. It was kind of like Tetris. I think I mentioned that.

Now, it turns out the next shift, and the one after that,
were also in the back room. After a few more shifts, I got
really, really good at shoebox organizing.

One day when I came in, I asked, again, if maybe they
might need me to sell some shoes on the sales floor. It turned
out that, yes, they did! . . . But not yet.

This went on for many weeks. I really wanted to learn to
interact with people. They said they would rather I work in the
back room. I asked about the referee shirt, and they told me
it was for the sales guys. That made sense, I guess. I wasn't a
sales guy. I was more of a Shoebox Organizing Guy. An S.O.G.

Eventually, I politely resigned. I never got my ref shirt. I
still want to get a ref shirt.

I saw a Help Wanted sign at a nearby pie restaurant. Maybe
I could be a waiter! I was already picturing myself interacting
successfully with people who wanted to order pie.

Once again, I made it through the interview. The Head Pie
Lady was impressed by my vocabulary, I think, and also my

hair. People respond favorably to my hair. If I could just send my hair out to socialize, I would do that.

There was no backroom start for me at the pie restaurant! I got a Pie-Full Delight apron and a hat, and the Head Pie Lady quickly trained me and assigned me some tables to work and briefed me on the quiche-and-pie menu. (Footnote: I genuinely still don't quite know what quiche is.)

It was noisy and crowded at lunchtime. Really noisy. And the busyness was overwhelming, disorienting, and chaotic. To give you a picture of what it was like, it reminded me of the busy city scene in *Blade Runner*, but it wasn't a city with lights and hordes of punk-rock future-people. It was more of a pie store.

I failed at being a waiter. Badly.

It turns out that to be a server you have to remember things. For example:

1. People and
2. The Things Those People Ordered.

I tried so hard, but I was confused and awful. The Head Pie Lady had mercy on me, so she assigned me to be the checkout guy.

Because of my head moving back and forth whenever I tried to enter the information, each customer in line thought I was saying, "No . . . no . . . no . . . ." to them. They would ask me what the problem was. I tried to explain to everyone that it was a medical condition. People wanted to know more. Every transaction became a discussion about neurology, which I thought was interesting, but it turns out the Head Pie Lady was more interested in me keeping the line moving.

Eventually—soon, actually—I was assigned to the back room. They didn't want to fire me. They felt bad, I think. They had me fold pie boxes back there and store them.

You know what? I was pretty good at it. It was kind of like Tetris.

In church you're supposed to get out there and "evangelize." Get out in the world, get out in the culture, just *get out there* and start talking to people excitedly about Jesus.

Francis Chan, a well-known pastor/author/evangelist, said talking about Jesus with friends, neighbors, and strangers shouldn't be all that hard:

> We love our kids. We'll talk about our kids all day. We love our wives. We'll talk about our wives. We love a sport. We'll talk about that sport. But when we talk about Jesus, it doesn't just flow out of this natural, this is who I am. I'm crazy about God and what He did for me. It's supernatural how He answers my prayers, and I just love Him.
>
> That type of conversation, I understand, is politically incorrect to talk that way, but nonetheless, I think the biggest problem in the church is this awkwardness. We just don't know how to converse with people. We're scared to do it, so we don't do it.[1]

Chan is right: Christians do get weird when they have to talk about Jesus. Maybe it's because Christians are induced to talk about Him out of guilt. Yes, it's often awkward to talk to people we don't know very well about *anything* out of guilt. We don't do that with other subjects. We've been taught that this, however, is The Thing All Christians Must Be Good At.

You might talk easily about the NBA, but suddenly, when it comes to Jesus, you switch from speaking naturally to speaking out of obligation to earn favor with God.

Yes, that's a prescription for weird.

I daresay even for people with actual social skills.

"We'll talk about our kids all day . . ." Not really. Honestly. Not all of us. I mean, you can get me started on my kids, if I know you, sure. But, no, it's not a natural thing for non-extroverts, not in most social environments, to easily talk at all.

(Except, perhaps, about a narrow topic of peculiar interest. It's true; I can talk about World War I for hours. Don't even get me started on the Battle of the Somme. But that's not the point.)

While Chan said church people get "awkward" when it comes to talking about Jesus, I can assure him that for many of us, the "awkward" part starts with just talking. In fact, the awkward precedes the talking.

> While Chan said church people get "awkward" when it comes to talking about Jesus, I can assure him that for many of us, the "awkward" part starts with just talking.

Awkward is a given. Awkward is a way of life.

I like Francis Chan a lot. I respect him, and I'm thankful for him. He's got a true gift for sharing the good news about Jesus with people.

And that's just it: it's a *gift*. Evangelism—the telling of the good news about Jesus—is described as a *gift* in the New Testament.

> Christ gave gifts to people—he made some to be apostles, some to be prophets, some to go and tell the Good News, and some to have the work of caring for and teaching God's people. (Eph. 4:11 NCV)

Growing up in church, I'd heard it said hundreds of times that evangelism was everybody's primary job in life. But when it came to other gifts on that same list—like, say, doing apostolic work—I didn't hear this.

So if I wasn't personally bringing people to Christ, or at least bringing new people to church, I was failing. I simply needed to be enthusiastically talking to people about Jesus in all sorts of settings, or at least have the decency to feel perpetually guilty for not doing it.

Imagine my shock, then, when I couldn't find this as a fundamental emphasis in the New Testament description of the church.

You'd think Paul would have filled his letters to the churches with evangelistic emphases, commands, encouragements, and advice, but it's just not there. Yes, Jesus tells His disciples to "Go into all the world . . ." to make disciples (Mark 16:15), and the Twelve did exactly that. But Paul doesn't seem to think this was a message intended in the same way for everyone. His letters to believers have almost nothing about this.

You know what *is* in those letters? A repeated, almost nonstop emphasis on how Christians should treat *each other*: reminders and instructions to be patient with each other; to submit to each other; to show hospitality to each other; to be at peace with each other; to forgive each other; to give preference to each other; to serve each other . . .

> Imagine my shock, then, when I couldn't find [evangelism] as a fundamental emphasis in the New Testament description of the church.

There simply aren't many directives on evangelism, but there sure is a lot about unity.

As it turns out, that is exactly what attracted people to the people of The Way in the first centuries. Maybe this shouldn't be a shock, given that Jesus prayed for unity and said it would be *the way that people would know we belonged to Him* (John 17:20–23).

Unity is job one. And we're all well equipped to do that. It's a wonderful thing. Our different temperaments, backgrounds, passions, gifts, abilities, and resources all add up to a beautiful mosaic.

Alan Kreider is one of the foremost historians on the early church, and he marvels at how the numbers of believers exploded in the first few centuries. It wasn't respectable to be a Christian, but people did it anyway. So why'd they do it?

He rules out public preaching, since there was very little of that. Too dangerous, he says. There weren't big organized plans for outreach either. There's no evidence that praying for conversions was a top priority, even though praying for enemies and persecutors clearly was central. Here's something else he calls "astonishing":

> To this list of surprising omissions I would like to add one more. In my reading of early Christian materials with a missionary's eyes, I have been amazed at the absence of pastoral admonitions to evangelise. A sample of this is *Ad Quirinum* by the North African bishop and martyr Cyprian. The third book of this work is a manual of 120 "heavenly precepts" to guide catechumens in the Christian life. These "precepts" cover a whole range of areas of Christian concern—"that brethren ought to support one another," or "that we are to be urgent in prayers"—but none, not one of the 120, urges the new believers to evangelise.[2]

This seems crazy, indeed. So why were so many drawn in, when being a Jesus-follower was dangerous? Kreider says it's because life together simply transformed people into people who acted like Jesus. It was very attractive, in a disordered culture of addictions with a widening gap between rich and poor, to see people who were truly free. They were modeling an alternative society, one that looked like the kingdom of God.

It was wildly appealing. "How," Kreider says people asked, "do Christians live like that?"

The pre-Christendom Christians sensed that they, by God's grace, had been ushered into a privileged place. The mid-third-century bishop of Carthage, Cyprian, repeatedly referred to it as an "enclosed garden":

> A garden: here is life flowering and flourishing in the presence of Christ. Cyprian and other Christians sought repeatedly to express the delight and the newness of their common life in Christ. "This is a new people, and there is something divine mingled with it." This is "a new race or way of life". This is "God's country". This is "Paradise". This is "the place where the Holy Spirit flourishes".
>
> The heart of the newness was the person and teaching of Jesus Christ.[3]

An "enclosed garden." Wow, do I like that. I'd never heard the church referred to that way. As an introvert, this has great appeal for me.

Clearly, it's not that it is locked to outsiders at all. It's that it's an alternative society, where people flourish by one-anothering. The net result is that the garden grows.

People want to be part of a culture that unites races, the rich and the poor, male and female, slave and free. We're all yearning for this.

And we can all be a part of it. We all get a role. We all get a place at the table, even introverts, whose "thing" isn't striking up conversations with strangers.

I still talk with people about Jesus, but here's what's odd: it's way more natural than it was when I thought it was my Solemn Duty and Primary Job Number One of being a Christian.

There used to be a TV show called *Pimp My Ride*, and I didn't feel cool enough to watch it, or even say it, but I watched it anyway.

There was this super-hip rapper guy who hosted it, and people with junky cars would get a complete car makeover by some guys in a garage. There was the painting guy and another guy who did upholstery. There was a stereo guy, and a wheels guy. Another guy did engines and mufflers and stuff.

They all had tats and high-fived a lot. I liked that. I don't have any tats, but I do like to high-five with humans.

Anyway, I remember one episode when this nerdy white guy brought in his pickup truck. They wound up installing a hydraulic table tennis table in it, because the nerdy guy was good at table tennis. Then they played doubles with him.

It made me think of the church and how we all have our "thing." Not everyone is an extroverted conversation starter. Not everyone is a wise counselor. Not everyone is naturally great at prayer or encouragement. Not everyone can fold pie boxes as well as I can, sure—my talent is jaw-droppingly freakish—but some people are gifted with mufflers. And we add all these talents together to be a blessing to people.

By design, God's family, the church, is a beautiful, messy, refreshing, and often very awkward thing. Thank You, Lord, for that. I don't know who said it first, but the church has been described as "H.C.E.": Here Comes Everybody. The whole motley lot of us, sprinting and jumping and limping and being wheeled and carried in on gurneys.

My friend Jacob is right there with us:

Looking back on my life, I can see that I dealt with anxiety from the time I was a child, particularly around spiritual things. From an early age I was terrified that if threatened with persecution, I wouldn't be able to stand strong in my faith, and thus I would go to hell.

As I learned about the "importance of evangelism," this anxiety expanded and increased. I also was very anxious over people's rejection, so I ended up feeling caught between two poles of debilitating anxiety. If I wasn't brave enough to overcome my fear of people's rejection, it meant I was ashamed of the gospel and would risk losing my salvation. But anxiety over people's rejection was crippling to the point of panic attacks.

Jacob isn't a spiritual failure, but he's been made to feel like one. As he knows now, he's simply an introvert, and a talented one at that. Jacob is an analyst for the FBI, who uses his intelligence and analytical gift to protect us from terrorism. We're not all gifted the same way. That's a beautiful thing.

Cool, uncool; outgoing, shy—shouldn't matter. I'm just glad you're part of us. And it's been that way since Jesus hand-picked His first followers.

Thank God. Here comes everybody, including you and me.

Blessed Are the People
Who Can't Pray Worth a Darn

LAST YEAR ALONE, CHRISTIAN PUBLISHERS RELEASED 1,482,889 books about prayer.

Perhaps that statistic shocks you, and it should, because I actually just made it up. But the point is people talk about prayer a lot, and not just in Christian circles. In fact, three out of four Americans say they pray regularly.[1] (I didn't make up that one.)

Everybody seems to talk about it. Every religious person believes in it, and even many of the nonreligious ones. Prayer is a big deal. It changes the world. There's power in prayer.

It's also a big guilt-trip for me, because I'm terrible at it. It's embarrassing. I'm in my forties. I always thought that I'd be good at this by now.

At risk of further humiliation (probably too late in the book to worry about that), here's my usual mental monologue during group prayer, when we close our eyes and people take turns jumping in with prayers.

Okay, Brant, focus on what this guy is saying. Yes, Lord, help his grandma who is sick with cancer. I've never met her, but, Lord, please be with her and I kind of miss my own grandma. She was pretty awesome. Oh man—she used to have Cocoa Krispies for us. Mom would never let us have that, but Grandma did and I love how they kinda turned the milk brown.

Or was that Cocoa Puffs? Do Cocoa Puffs turn the milk brown? Man, I'd love to have me some Cocoa Puffs. So good. Or Cookie Crisp! That stuff was crazy-good, and it was like pouring milk over a bowl of cookies for breakfast. Wow . . .

And, Lord, please help the lady who's praying right now and her aunt who also has cancer. That's gotta be horrible. Lord, I feel so bad I don't know that praying lady's name. Sharla? Shireen? Something like that. My sister-in-law is named Sharla. I wonder how she's doing. I love what she and my brother named their cat: Chairman Meow. That's the best. Chairman Meow.

Chairman Meow is so funny.

Next time I name a cat, I want to find something like that. Some kind of historical reference. Like that zoo that named the camel Alexander Camelton. That's so awesome, and okay, it's silent now. What's going on?

Are they waiting on me?

Okay, I'm going to pray out loud here, about something. Quick: Who do I know who's in the hospital? Maybe I'll pray about something else. I don't know. I'd like to just thank God for stuff, but now I'm all in my head. Am I praying so other people can hear me, or am I actually talking to God? I don't want to pray out loud if it's just so others can hear. But maybe that's okay. I don't know. I guess I'll clear my throat and start and—

Okay. Steve started.

Cool. God, we thank You for whatever Steve is talking about, and oh wow I guess we're wrapping up inJesusnameamen.

Prayer time finished. Someone says something about how powerful it was and how they could sense God's presence. I again wonder why God doesn't give up on me and my flittering, faithless mind.

Here's where it's helpful for me to remember something. Something really good.

When God became a man, when He took on flesh and walked among us, He stood in front of a crowd and told them how to pray in Matthew 6. The crowd lived in a religion-soaked culture, wherein lengthy public prayers were the order of the day and were associated with rightness with God.

Jesus says, "Here's how to pray . . ." and *He then prays for about twenty-five seconds.*

And then quits!

I've timed it. I realize I'm reading the English version of verses 9–13, but I doubt the Aramaic took much longer. We have no reason to believe Jesus used long pauses, either, to stretch it out. Why would He? He'd already blasted people for lengthy public prayers. He told them to quit blathering on and on.

> Jesus says, "Here's how to pray . . ." and *He then prays for about twenty-five seconds.* And then quits!

So God Himself told us how to pray, and it's incredibly short.

This strikes me as more than just instructive, more than corrective, and more than ironic.

For people like me and maybe you, if you're terrible at prayer, it's just beautiful. And merciful. And understanding. Even tender.

It's like God already knows about our fluttering little minds. He knows we're like little birds, easily distracted little things, and the weak among us still really do want to be part of His kingdom.

Twenty-five seconds.

As it turns out, that's about all I have before my mind starts to drift.

Embarrassing? Yes. But I'm not alone. I took a very unscientific poll on my Twitter account asking people about this. And with more than nine hundred responses, the overwhelming majority said their minds start to drift in the first minute of prayer.

I want you to know, if you're like me, that God understands, and still wants us at His party.

Jesus said, "Pray like this!"—and He kept it short.

This is a God who knows us and loves us, indeed.

So let's talk about prayer, even for people like me, the Worst Pray-er Ever: I'm convinced a bumbling, fumbling ten-second prayer is a million times better than no prayer at all. Here's why:

In Praise of the Ten-Second Prayer

1. It forces me into humility. By praying even for a fleeting moment, I'm acknowledging two fundamental truths: First, I'm not God. Someone Else is.

2. ... And, second, yes, it's a Someone. Not an impersonal Life Force that has no personality or will of its own. He is other. Different. I'm not praying to myself or to gravity or to magnetism.

3. It's great *because* it's so hard for me to do. I'm doing it, despite all my doubts and hesitations and issues and hang-ups and tendency to be easily distracted, because I believe God is "worth" it. That means my little, measly prayer is an act of—get this—genuine worship.

4. What we say in those ten seconds actually matters. God wants our interaction, and even though I often feel like I'm talking into dead air, things happen. Odd things. Merciful things. I've seen it.

5. It reminds me I'm part of a larger story. A way bigger, better, and even real-er story. And that reminder helps me rewrite my lesser stories, the substitute ones, about how it's all about me, and what people think of me, and my own struggle for significance. The bigger story is better.

So, yes, for me ten seconds is way better than zero. Apparently, what God is really after is my heart. Ten seconds says, "God, this heart is broken, faithless, and distracted, but yep—it's Yours."

I think He likes that.

I've found, too, that the ten-second prayer actually happens, while the wait-for-the-perfect-setting half-hour prayer doesn't. I just looked up images for "prayer" online, and found lots of sunrays. People on their knees, silhouetted against the morning sun; people standing on a hill with a cross, with the sun setting behind them; people with hands folded, with sunrays emanating from their heads.

I've found if I wait for awesome prayer-y settings, or for sunrays to emanate from my own head, I don't pray at all. If I think a legitimate prayer must be at least ten minutes, I don't pray at all. If I think God is angry at me because I haven't been praying enough, I don't pray at all.

Guilt about praying doesn't help me pray. Freedom helps me pray. Believing God's not incensed at me helps me pray. Believing God is okay with my ten-second prayers helps me pray.

And you know what? Sometimes those prayers make it beyond ten seconds. But that's not the point. The point is now my "relationship with God" is actually a relationship with God.

I'm struck, too, by what that relationship can look like. Again, the version of God that I operate with in my mind— thanks to my upbringing, or my own lack of imagination—doesn't jibe with the actual God of the Bible, who's far more interesting.

In my mind's eye God is all-knowing, unapproachable, distinctly un-human, and operates according to a strict logic. In other words, He's something like the MacBook I'm currently using to type this sentence. There's no way I can relate to that. Given that understanding, I can't even fathom why He would want me to talk to Him, let alone ask Him for something He already knows I want or need.

But this isn't the God of the Bible at all. This God, Yahweh, is shocking. He doesn't just allow us to talk to Him; He lets us talk Him into things. For example, in Genesis 18, He allows Abraham to bargain with Him after God decided to destroy Sodom and Gomorrah. Think about how odd this exchange is, between a sinful man and God:

> Abraham approached him and said, "Will you sweep away both the righteous and the wicked? Suppose you find fifty righteous people living there in the city—will you still sweep it away and not spare it for their sakes? Surely you wouldn't do such a thing, destroying the righteous along with the wicked. Why, you would be treating the righteous and the wicked exactly the same! Surely you wouldn't do that! Should not the Judge of all the earth do what is right?"
>
> And the LORD replied, "If I find fifty righteous people in Sodom, I will spare the entire city for their sake."
>
> Then Abraham spoke again. "Since I have begun, let me speak further to my Lord, even though I am but dust and ashes. Suppose there are only forty-five righteous people rather than fifty? Will you destroy the whole city for lack of five?"
>
> And the LORD said, "I will not destroy it if I find forty-five righteous people there."
>
> Then Abraham pressed his request further. "Suppose there are only forty?"
>
> And the LORD replied, "I will not destroy it for the sake of the forty."
>
> "Please don't be angry, my Lord," Abraham pleaded. "Let me speak—suppose only thirty righteous people are found?"
>
> And the LORD replied, "I will not destroy it if I find thirty."
>
> Then Abraham said, "Since I have dared to speak to the Lord, let me continue—suppose there are only twenty?"

> And the LORD replied, "Then I will not destroy it for the sake of the twenty."
>
> Finally, Abraham said, "Lord, please don't be angry with me if I speak one more time. Suppose only ten are found there?"
>
> And the LORD replied, "Then I will not destroy it for the sake of the ten."
>
> When the LORD had finished his conversation with Abraham, he went on his way, and Abraham returned to his tent. (Gen. 18:23–33 NLT)

The cartoonish God of my imagination would never let someone get lawyerly with Him like that. He'd make up His mind instantly and do what He wants. No way does He have this conversation, and then go "on his way" after a "conversation." There would be no "conversation."

And yet, this is the actual God of the Bible. He wants conversation. He's even open to bargaining. Maybe this all seems irreverent and impossible to you, and it seems that way to me too. But I'm trying to align my faulty, simplistic idea of God with the God Who Actually Is.

I'm trying to align my faulty, simplistic idea of God with the God Who Actually Is.

Some people believe in God, but just can't bring themselves to believe He actually cares about us. Yet here's Jesus, telling a story that still shocks people. It's about a woman who won't quit until she gets her way:

"There was a judge in a certain city," he said, "who neither feared God nor cared about people. A widow of that city came to him repeatedly, saying, 'Give me justice in this dispute with my enemy.' The judge ignored her for a while, but finally he said to himself, 'I don't fear God or care about people, but this woman is driving me crazy. I'm going to see that she gets justice, because she is wearing me out with her constant requests!'" (Luke 18:2–5 NLT)

If I were inventing a God, there's no way I would have thought to make this something He would say: "Go ahead and hassle me. It works." And yet that's effectively what Jesus was saying:

Then the Lord said, "Learn a lesson from this unjust judge. Even he rendered a just decision in the end. So don't you think God will surely give justice to his chosen people who cry out to him day and night? Will he keep putting them off? I tell you, he will grant justice to them quickly!" (vv. 6–8 NLT)

You might be thinking, *Brant, that's not how God works. He knows everything, so we don't need to pester Him. The point of this story is not that we should always pray and never give up.* Okay, but this is how the story starts in verse 1:

One day Jesus told his disciples a story to show that they should always pray and never give up. (NLT)

So there's that.

Jesus Christ Himself is saying the Creator of earth and heaven, the almighty God, the Alpha and Omega . . . wants to be pestered. Sure, I may not be great at praying, but pestering? I'm a rock star at that.

It makes you wonder about God: What kind of father wants to be pestered? Probably one who really loves his children and is hoping they don't wait until the perfect moment, or until they are perfect themselves, before they finally talk to him.

Blessed Are the People Who Just Read That Last Chapter but Still Have Some Questions

THERE'S AN OBVIOUS CONCERN ABOUT PRAYER, particularly for those prone to doubt: *Why pray if God already knows what we need? What's more, if He knows of something that needs done, why doesn't He just do it?*

C. S. Lewis addressed this in an essay called "The Efficacy of Prayer": It's not about the "power of prayer," as though it were a magical incantation. Prayer is communicating with a real Person. Someone who doesn't believe in God might feel better after praying or meditating, but without someone on the other end of a request, someone with the ability to grant it or deny it, there is no real "power of prayer" at all.

Let's put it this way: I might pick up my iPhone to order a pizza and feel great about doing it. But if no one is actually on the other end of the line, there's no pizza coming. (The fact that Lewis did not use this example is, I'm sure, due to his era, not my lack of poetic imagination.)

And if God could go ahead and "fix it" without our prayers, without our communication with Him, we can say the same thing about anything we do, like feeding the hungry:

> It is not really stranger, nor less strange, that my prayers should affect the course of events than that my other actions should do so. They have not advised or changed God's mind—that is, His over-all purpose. But that purpose will be realized in different ways according to the actions, including the prayers, of His creatures.[1]

For reasons I can't fully understand, God allows me to play a role in restoring the world. He apparently is delighted when I love others instead of myself and care for them. He lets me do things that otherwise would not get done. My actions matter.

For further reasons I can't fully understand, God wants to be with me. He wants me to talk to Him. He wants me to open up to Him. He wants me to be honest. He wants me to ask Him for things. My prayers themselves are actions, and my actions matter.

Whenever a tragedy or horrible crime hits the news, there are two predictable reactions, one following from the other: First, there's a hashtag, like #prayforDallas. And then there's a response to that hashtag: "We don't need prayer. Enough with the prayers. We need ACTION!"

I understand the frustration, and were I a nonbeliever, I might respond the same way. But it's odd to see even fellow believers tweeting this sort of thing, as though prayer and "action" were at odds. We should know otherwise.

Now, someone might substitute tweeting a "#prayfor" for actual prayer, that's true. But if we believe Jesus, communicating with God is hardly at odds with making a real-world difference. He says we should ask God for things because He loves us.

Here's yet another consideration: perhaps you've seen, as I have, that prayer genuinely changes your own disposition toward others. It helps with perspective. This should matter, when our own thoughts and doubts suggest that what's needed isn't prayer, but action. Action, yes; but rightly ordered action, informed by wisdom and compassion.

Prayer, much as I'd like to avoid talking about it because I'm horrible at it, does change things. And the first thing it changes is my heart.

I don't think there are many ways to fail at praying besides not praying.

Not communicating is the problem. Yes, some of our prayers are clumsy

> I get the impression from Scripture that God would rather be in communication with an immature, selfish person than be ignored by a theologically fastidious one.

or meandering or even immature and selfish, but I get the impression from Scripture that God would rather be in communication with an immature, selfish person than be ignored by a theologically fastidious one.

I've had radio listeners ask me about how to stay awake during their prayers at night. They lie in bed and pray, and next thing they know, they're asleep. They feel guilty about that.

I told them I don't think they should feel guilty about that.

I'm a dad, and when my little son or daughter drifted off to sleep talking to me, I wasn't hurt or angry at all.

I was honored.

By the way, a digression about sleep: I love God's sense of humor. We humans get proud, all of us. We tend to think we're the captains of our own ships. We are the Masters of Our Destinies! We are in control! We know what we're doing! We're . . . we're . . .

. . . really tired and need to lie . . . down . . .

Zzzzzzzzzz.

Yes, it's true: we're actually designed to fall over, usually once every time Earth rotates, and curl up. Usually with a blankie.

Like—you know—a child.

Like a child who needs reminding she's not so in command after all. Or maybe like an adult who needs a refresher: you, Mr. Independent . . . are made of dust.

So I'm thankful for sleep. Every day, busy, busy, busy making decisions, calling shots, bearing the burdens of the day, stressed about this and that and what will I do about this? What about that? What if—? And what about—?

And then God makes me lie down. I must not be such a Big

Deal. I must not be Manager of Everything, because, shoot, I can't even manage being *vertical* anymore.

Proverbs says to ask for wisdom. Wisdom means perspective. It means knowing what matters. Ask for wisdom, Proverbs says, and this will happen:

> When you lie down, you will not be afraid;
> when you lie down, your sleep will be sweet. (3:24)

So yes, I loved it when my kids, after a day of frenetic playing and running about, fell asleep in the car. I'd get to pick them up and carry them to bed. The kid's out of gas, limp, trusting, completely vulnerable, and totally surrendered.

Fathers like that kind of stuff.

———

John Piippo is an author and philosophy professor who writes extensively about prayer. He appeals to me because he's not an emotional type either. He's logical. What he writes tends to make sense to me.

He says God is patient with us, and when our minds drift during prayer, there's something we can and should do: we should return to our prayer, but make our prayer about whatever it is that our minds keep drifting toward. That's because, apparently, it's the thing that truly matters to us. So why not share it?

Perhaps it's work. Maybe it's romance. Or it could be fearfulness about something. Maybe it's child-raising, or our own continual need for significance, or how slighted we feel about what that coworker said about us today. In any event, whatever it is that is occupying us is precisely what we should be talking to God about.

This may be obvious to you, but it was revelatory for me. I'm often ashamed of what's actually on my mind, the surface-level, often selfish nature of it all. God wants me to talk to Him about that?

Why do I resist doing this? It's as if I think I can hide it from God, or that He's naïve about what's really going on in my head.

It's like I'm afraid to be truly known. It could be that deep down and after all, that's actually my biggest "problem" with prayer.

Maybe it's the same reason I struggle so much to say "I love you" to people I truly love. I've never understood why it's so difficult. Some people never stop saying it. It flows out of them. But it's a battle for me. Yet I really do love people. I not only need them, I *know* I need them. Maybe I'm afraid to come face-to-face with how intense that truth really is.

Maybe the lack of sensing God's presence isn't the deepest cause of my struggle to pray. Like saying "I love you" and meaning it, maybe

> It's like I'm afraid to be truly known. It could be that deep down and after all, that's actually my biggest "problem" with prayer.

real prayer opens me up to a vulnerability that scares me. I don't know.

If I'm used to keeping my emotional distance and entering into relationships on those terms, well, that approach won't fly in real prayer. There's no fooling God.

If I begin to believe in my own innocence or that "everyone else is the problem," honest prayer interrupts the fantasy. I might be able to get away with that kind of immature thinking in my daily walking-around life, but if I'm aware I'm actually talking to God, this attitude becomes nakedly wrong. I can't fool Him.

If I want to ignore habits and selfish patterns of thinking, and if I want to protect them in the seeming privacy of my mind, prayer is a simply terrible idea.

Yes, I struggle to pray in part because I don't get an emotional reward. Maybe you're like that too.

But maybe my biggest problem isn't that prayer isn't real enough. Maybe it forces me to be all too real, when I'd rather hide.

TEN

Blessed Are the Wounded

I DON'T LIKE THE MEMOIR GENRE, THE LET-ME-TELL-you-all-the-evil-things-they-did-to-me   kind   of   memoir, anyway. This is because the past is, of course, the past. We can't be defined by it. And as a wise friend once told me, "As important as our childhoods are, childhood is still a relatively short time, a relatively long time ago."

It's not who we are anymore. Yes, childhood is formative, but for the humble, childhood is not the only formative period. We grow up. We keep learning.

We resolve not to repeat the mistakes of our parents, and all of our parents have made mistakes. We can even be thankful (and I am) for what we've endured.

The mess can make for something beautiful.

Maybe God is like one of those Food Network master chefs, on one of those shows where they give cooks some random, odd ingredients and then challenge them to make a gourmet meal out of them. ("Okay, here's halibut, a gourd, and a Hostess Ding Dong. Go.")

He apparently specializes in making something of nothing. Maybe He also enjoys making something truly beautiful out of worse than nothing.

I write this not so that you'll marvel at my circumstances—they're not marvelous—but because you might relate; or, if you don't, maybe you'll have insight into why others see and experience God differently.

Some come by faith easily. Others of us are constantly squinting, constantly skeptical, constantly asking, *Is that true . . . ?*

If that's you, please know I understand. If it's not you, I hope you can be patient with us. We could all use more patience.

———

My dad was a Bible preacher. He still is.

I love him. We get along just fine. He's in his seventies and spends his time playing guitar and singing for old folks in nursing homes. In that way, he's a blessing to people who are often ignored. I like that.

We've always liked to sing. At one point, our family (my dad and mom and my older brother, Darin, and me) even had a quartet. We sang Southern Gospel, four-part-harmony style. We had our own microphones with different colored windscreens on them. I think mine was green. I'm glad there are apparently no surviving videos of this.

Dad is a forceful preacher. He's a big man, too, with a booming voice. I thought I'd grow up to be his size, but I'm still waiting. I'm five feet ten, and he's several inches taller and remains an imposing presence. He's always been a church minister too. Even for the short periods when he wasn't full time (I remember his stints driving a cab and selling brushes door-to-door), he would get fill-in jobs preaching.

He held full-time minister jobs in small towns all over Illinois and Indiana. He would be the preacher at a country church for about a year and then find another place he'd rather be, and we'd move again.

He preached a lot—three times a week: Sunday mornings, Sunday evenings, and Wednesday nights too. I was raised on preaching and talk of preaching and preachers.

We belonged to a fundamental church that was proudly Bible-based, and proudly nondenominational. And by "nondenominational" I mean, of course, "denominational," because we thought we were the only ones who really, truly understood the Bible. We'd only do things with other churches that belonged to our specific non-denomination.

We believed we were in the right about key doctrinal issues, and everyone else was probably . . . well, you know . . . going to hell. Presbyterians, Methodists, Catholics . . . all misled, all lost. I say "probably" going to hell, because we held out hope that God's boundless mercy might—*might*—extend all the way to Baptists.

Maybe. We'll see.

I knew how to do church. While other kids were playing firefighter (or whatever normal kids do), Darin and I were playing church, arguing over who got to have the spotlight as preacher. Darin would preach at me from Romans chapter 5, verse 1, and then sit there while I'd preach at him from . . . Romans chapter 5, verse 1.

I'm still not sure why it was always that verse, but man, we had Romans 5:1 down.

Real-life church wasn't just three times a week either. We'd frequently have to clean ourselves up and comb our hair for weeklong revivals.

Revivals were when we'd shake up the usual Sunday-morning hymns-and-preaching formula by meeting each weeknight for some hymns and some preaching. Sometimes we'd get a little crazy and have hymns, preaching . . . and then more hymns.

So, while we'd normally have to sit through three sermons a week, sometimes we got seven or eight.

People really liked my dad's preaching and singing. My brother and I were often told what a wonderful man he was.

We were also absolutely petrified of him.

Honestly, I still don't know what happened to him, or when. There are a lot of things I don't want to remember. I recall bits and pieces, like being four years old, in a fast-moving car late at night, while my mom drove my preacher dad to the hospital. He was in the back seat, breathing into a paper bag.

I remember late-night yelling matches. I remember my mom yelling, "Who is she? Tell me who she is!" over and over.

I remember visiting Dad over the years, through grade school and middle school, in psychiatric wards and mental institutions. When you visit your dad in these places, it makes an impression on you. When you see him preaching days later, you remember that too.

I remember our bathroom floors. Very well. I'd sit there, sometimes for hours. I'd make up stories to distract myself from the arguing. Sometimes I would bring my favorite puppet, a little furry green monster, with me (I was big on puppets), and I'd sit and act out little sketches.

That was the coping plan. Go somewhere and lock the door and sit on the floor and rock back and forth and make up a puppet story or just try not to exist.

I remember Darin and me watching a tiny television in our shared room in one of the small-town, church-owned parsonages we lived in. We were watching reruns of *Gilligan's Island*, with the volume at full blast to try to cover up the escalating conflict. I remember Darin darting off quickly to the kitchen, gathering up all the sharp knives, and returning to our room, where we sat with them, violently shaking, eyes glued on the television.

I remember going back to church and listening to more Bible-based preaching from my dad, and then remembering we would have to go home soon and feeling like I'd been punched in the gut. I didn't want to be at church listening to him. But I sure didn't want to go home.

I remember my brother heroically intervening in my parents' room when Dad was beginning to physically attack my mom. She thought she was going to die, she said. I remember her telling Darin, "I think you saved my life."

I remember thinking my older brother was a hero. (I still think so, honestly.) He's even smaller than I am, and standing up to Dad had to be intimidating.

I remember being told what a wonderful family we were. I remember hearing, so many times, "Your dad is such a great man of God."

I remember walking home from school, happy that the day had gone well and the sun was out, and then praying I wouldn't see my dad's car in the parsonage driveway when I got home. *Please don't be home. I just want peace.*

I remember more revivals, more preaching, more Bible studies, more outreach programs, more talk of Bible-this and Bible-that. More Bible camps. This is the life of the Bible preacher's kid.

I remember one frightening night, quickly jumping in a car with my mom and my brother to escape from our home. My teeth were literally chattering. I couldn't make them stop. I even remember thinking, *So this really happens when you're super-scared. Your teeth actually do this.*

I remember sitting in the living room, again watching TV with my brother, another evening as my parents argued. My dad angrily left, slammed the door to the garage, started the car, and went forward instead of backward, smashing into the wall directly behind the TV we were facing. My brother and I started screaming and rushed for the outside door.

We thought we were about to be run over by a car . . . in our living room.

I remember—vividly—reaching for the front door lock, trying to unlock it, watching my own shaking hands as we screamed, trying to get out of the way.

It was then that I had an epiphany: *I'm not going to let anything bother me anymore.* And I suddenly stopped crying.

Stopped feeling.

I *decided* to quit feeling things. That was the moment. I can still see the door handle. I can still see my shaking hand.

And I can still see it stop shaking.

I remember my parents' first divorce. Dad moved out of town, and we weren't allowed to stay in our house since it was the church parsonage. We had to leave. I felt ashamed. Everyone knew our story. My mom bought a very old, five-hundred-square-foot house for $9,000.

I remember, months later, playing catch with a friend. I turned to go home and saw our house, and Dad's green Chevy out front. I didn't want to go in.

I walked in, and he sat us down and told us he had important news. He had been diagnosed with leukemia. He was sobbing. He had six months to live.

I couldn't believe it. I'd decided not to let anyone affect me anymore.

But I didn't know how to react. I looked at my brother, and he started crying. I started bawling. For all the heartbreak and tension and fear we'd known, this was a new nightmare: our dad was dying!

Except he wasn't. Weeks later, he admitted it was a lie. He'd wanted attention.

Still, my mom was eventually convinced that he was "better," that he'd turned his life around, and that whatever mental illnesses he'd struggled with were in the past. He'd sought counseling, and he was taking the right medication. She just wanted her family to work. She wanted a dad for her boys. I understood that.

But I didn't believe him. I wanted peace. I remember lying in bed, asking her to please reconsider the idea of marrying him again.

I remember being the ring bearer in my parents' second wedding. I was twelve or thirteen. I stood in the outdoor ceremony, in my new light-brown suit, and wished I could go in a room, lock the door, and sit on the floor and rock back and forth.

I don't recall much about the marriage after that, except a couple more moves and more tension. And then I remember riding around town with my brother, who was newly licensed at sixteen. I was fourteen. We saw a friend from church named Jon out mowing his lawn. We pulled up alongside him.

I remember sitting in the front seat, staring out the window, thinking about playing basketball or something since it was a beautiful day. And then my brother, hand on the steering wheel, casually telling Jon, who was leaning on his push mower: "Yeah, my parents are getting divorced again."

That was the first I'd heard of it.

I turned to stare at the floor mat.

I didn't say anything.

I didn't feel anything either.

I love my dad.

That may sound dissonant to some, after sharing this story, but it's true, and my brother loves him too. We want the best for him. We always have.

I've had to deal with a great deal of anger, but there's no use harboring it. Forgiveness helps everybody, and what's more, we don't have a choice if we have any desire to live a Jesus-shaped life. (I wrote a book about that, actually, and how we must forgive and drop our anger, no matter what.[1] Some of the reaction I got: "Clearly you've never been through any difficulty in life, so . . .")

My dad says he wants to "finish strong," and I believe that is exactly what he is doing.

He'd like a do-over, and so would we all. He even wants me to share this story. I wouldn't do it without his blessing. He's been an excellent grandpa to our kids. He owns up to the past, and he wants people to know how God, using hard lessons, can change people.

I've often told him I'm thankful now for the past, and that includes the absurdity and the hurt. My dad has his own hurts, unsurprisingly from his parents. (For starters, his strictly religious mom used to routinely threaten that his misbehavior would cause her to die in the night, and he would feel guilty in the morning. Parenting Tip: Don't do that.)

Maybe his past was the perfect recipe to yield a very guilt-ridden, broken, God-haunted country preacher. Maybe my past was the perfect recipe to yield a very wounded, very skeptical man.

But maybe this is also a recipe for The Great Chef Who Likes a Challenge to yield someone who can still be a blessing to people somehow.

That kid who sat on the floor in the locked bathroom and made up stories? Now his actual job is Storyteller for CURE International. Seriously. I even use my puppets in the children's wards at CURE's hospitals. So it's ALL paying off . . .

> Maybe my past was the perfect recipe to yield a very wounded, very skeptical man.

Henri Nouwen was a Catholic priest, accomplished writer, and Harvard and Yale professor, who spent the last decade of his life serving people with profound disabilities. He wrote this near the end of his life.

> Nobody escapes being wounded. We are all wounded people, whether physically, emotionally, mentally, or spiritually. The main question is not, "How can we hide our wounds?" so we don't have to be embarrassed, but "How can we put our woundedness in the service of others?" When our wounds cease to be a source of shame, and become a source of healing, we have become wounded healers.[2]

Once there was a man who needed healing. He'd been unable to walk for thirty-eight years. When Jesus met him, He asked the man a seemingly odd question: "Do you *want* to be healed?" (John 5:6 ESV, emphasis added).

I'm a wounded man. I know that. I've seen, too, how wounded people hurt others. I know I'm more than capable of this if I refuse to forgive and continually rehearse the wrongs that have been done to me. You and I are free to spend the remainder of our days reacting to the hurts of our past.

But if we want to experience God in a different way, start something new, and be a blessing to people, we have to want to be healed.

Yes, the wounds are real, but you know what? Healing is real too.

Blessed Are Those Who Don't Have Amazing Spiritual Stories

AND SO HERE WE ARE IN THE MESSY MEANTIME.
This bugs some people, including me, because I hate "To Be Continued . . ."

I was going to explain why, but contemporary philosopher Jerry Seinfeld does it better than I can:

> It's horrible when you sense the "To Be Continued . . ." coming. You know, you're watching the show, you're into the story, and there's like five minutes left and suddenly you realize, "Hey, they can't make it! Timmy's still stuck in the cave! There's no way they wrap this up in five minutes!"
>
> I mean, the whole reason you watch a TV show is because it ends. If I wanted a long, boring story with no point to it, I have my life.[1]

Exactly. We don't ask much from our *Brady Bunch* reruns, really, except to please wrap everything up in thirty minutes.

Don't leave us hanging, wondering if they can escape after being locked in a jail cell on their family vacation. Please resolve this. Right now.

We after-school TV-watchers are not the first to grapple with this. Apparently, when Mozart was a little kid, he had to have resolution too.

The story goes that he was in bed upstairs and someone was playing the piano, and that someone got distracted and stopped, just before the last chord.

Wolfgang couldn't stand it. He tromped downstairs, pounded out the resolving chord, and then went back up to bed again, without a word. He just had to hear it.

I think we're all like that.

I think about all the stories I've heard, and then the ones I've lived, and there's a big difference: we get resolution in the former, but the others just . . . lie . . . out there somewhere, and much as we pretend, there are no finish lines, no final chords, no official victories, no ends-of-story.

Not yet, anyway.

Seinfeld's right: real life doesn't work quite like that. You may hear people tell "testimony" stories and get the impression that God is at work in other people's lives in a dramatically different way than He works in yours. Maybe He is, and maybe He isn't. In church culture a lot of half stories get told.

And then there are the stories we don't tell. We mostly keep them to ourselves, because we don't quite know what to do with them.

I took the yellow bus home from our country school in St. Bernice, Indiana. One day I sat with my friend Jeffrey. He was in second grade; I was in third. We talked and joked about my lunchbox and my furry green puppet, the one I brought with me everywhere.

Then we both got off at the usual bus stop in front of his house and said good-bye.

I stepped to the right. But Jeffrey ran alongside the bus, waving at our friends. He slipped.

He fell under the wheel.

Two weeks later, my mom suggested I go over to Jeffrey's house to visit his brother and his little sister. They hadn't been back to school, and Mom told me they likely hadn't had any visitors since Jeffrey was killed. They were probably lonely, she said.

My mom was right. They were very lonely. The two of them, also grade-school kids, met me at the door. They were excited to see me. We laughed and played with a top on their hardwood floor. It was one of those that spins and makes noise and has little lights.

I could see their mom in the back room, smoking a cigarette. Glaring at me.

We played for an hour and then she came in the room. She was screaming. I didn't understand what was happening. She was screaming at me. She said something about how all I was doing was reminding them of what happened to Jeffrey and I should get out right now.

Her kids were stunned, and they started crying, and so did I, and then I ran out the door and all the way home bawling with guilt.

I never went back. And we moved away. I don't know what happened to them. When I think about that day—this was decades ago—I still get a knot in my stomach.

What's the ending to this story? What's the moral?

I don't know. I honestly don't.

So it's not a story I often tell.

Most examples aren't this painful, but almost all the stories of my life are this way. They don't wrap up easily.

So when I speak to people and I try to motivate them, or teach them, or just make a point I like to make, I pull a bit of a sleight of hand, presenting stories that are edited just so. They're not "untrue"; they're just subtly not quite honest, because I'm presenting incomplete, messy, real-life stories like they're *Aesop's Fables*, with certain resolution as though the story were over.

Anyone who's been around American churches is used to the "And that's when she found the Lord!" stories, but they don't often include, "But, yeah, she's still battling addictions, like the rest of us."

I read "Look what our awesome church is doing!" accounts on church websites, but don't read any messy follow-ups. We get the "victory" stories over sin and depravity, but no one publishes books called *Whoops, I'm Totally Messed Up Again.*

That's where the stories of our actual lives are. But we don't like our stories open-ended.

So we clean up our stories and act like they're finished.

And we clean up ourselves and act like we're finished.

When I worked with teenagers at a church, I'd occasionally go to youth ministry conferences. They were packed with impressive youth ministers, one after the other telling us remarkable stories about what happened in their youth groups. It was really amazing! But why was my youth group kind of a mess? Why wasn't I inspiring anyone like that? It was impressive! . . . Until I realized I could pick and choose stories from my own group, make believe they were final, and, presto—I'm impressive.

I had good stories too. Like that inspiring day on the mission trip when Big Joe the Offensive Lineman cried and prayed and his life was changed forever. What a great ending.

Except I leave out the part where he got a girl pregnant a few months later.

Maybe we're not lying exactly, but cumulatively these stories can give people an expectation for life that's rarely met.

You know what? I even did the not-quite-the-full-story thing in my last book.

I wrote about a friend of mine named Michael, who inspired me by using his coffee shop to demonstrate a radical, Jesus-centered hospitality to people of all backgrounds. I wrote about how he represented Jesus so beautifully. I wrote about how he loved people so well.

Oh, it's all true. Everything I wrote.

What I did not write about is how he killed himself a few years later.

Michael had always struggled with addiction. We all knew it, even if we didn't want to admit it.

He was always giving, and I was always accepting. He even helped me drive my family's moving truck as we moved away from him, from Illinois to Texas. The long conversations in the truck made it obvious: he was feeling overwhelmed by life, even by his wonderful new wife and baby.

So when I heard he'd moved out of his house, away from his wife, and no one could reach him, I wasn't completely shocked.

And months later I picked up the phone and heard the news.

Was I dishonest, leaving this out? I don't know. I don't think so, but I don't know. I didn't know how to write it. I also didn't want to struggle, again, with wondering if I was a good enough friend. I wrote about him because I wanted to make a point about the time I saw a man loving people in a way that reminded me of Jesus.

Michael did that beautifully.

So you want a true story? One of the most loving, Christ-centered people I've ever seen in action . . . killed himself in an old motel room.

That doesn't make for a good sermon illustration. But it's life on earth.

Half stories are cleaner, and I guess they're useful. We can't include everything all the time.

The danger, of course, is that if we reside only in the Land of Half Stories, we don't get a sense of how good God actually is. When we compare ourselves to them, we may only see how messy we remain, without realizing He's using us in spite of it all.

Maybe this is why Jesus' stories are metaphors. Maybe you noticed He rarely picked individual people and didn't name anyone to make His point. He never said, "Let me tell you about that time that Andrew here was really awesome and helped an old lady across the street and . . ."

I suspect He refrained from doing that because He knows us so well. He knows we'd instantly start missing the point and worshiping The Perfect Andrew and reenacting The Holy Crossing of the Street in yearly festivals.

> The danger, of course, is that if we reside only in the Land of Half Stories, we don't get a sense of how good God actually is.

We'd compare ourselves to The Perfect Andrew and find ourselves hopelessly wanting. We'd be ashamed, perhaps without even admitting it, and maybe we'd slink away.

So instead we get parables featuring fictional people.

The greatest storyteller of all time refused to name names. He knew we'd instantly presume the hero of His story exists on a higher spiritual plane than we do. And He never, ever allows that. He does just the opposite. (Recall Matthew 23 where Jesus basically says, "You're all my students. I'm your teacher.")

The stories about actual humans who populate the real-life

stories in the Bible—they don't fit Sunday school lessons. That is, they only fit if you cut them in half. We like highlights. We like to keep the spectacular stuff, and the other parts wind up on the editing room floor.

In Sunday school I heard about Elijah, and how he had a showdown with the priests of a false god. He challenged them, and he won, big-time. Elijah's God made it obvious who the real one was. It was dramatic and public and final. Mic drop. High fives. End of lesson.

Except the Bible, for its part, doesn't let us stop there. Elijah went into a big depression, and if you think the highly public showdown and blowout victory would make Elijah have a come-to-Yahweh moment, you're wrong. He asked God to take his life. He felt that low.

This will seem odd to some, but knowing we're all currently a mess, in our own ways, isn't depressing to me.

It's freeing. Because it says God can still use me. He hasn't given up on me. Whatever I am—too this, too that—He still wants me to be part of His story, which, we're promised, does have an ultimate resolution.

Maybe your life seems confusing and messy because you're human. Perhaps God is not shocked by this, and uses us anyway to do profound, courageous, and beautiful things.

An early Christian referred to himself, repeatedly, as "the worst of sinners" (1 Tim. 1:16), and he did it while he was writing much of what is now the New Testament. Paul didn't write, "I used to be a really bad guy, but now I'm a good guy." He was saying, "I am the worst," present tense.

Think about that: Here's a man who was not a worldly success. He wasn't rich. He was occasionally a prisoner. He also admitted he was *currently* a horrible sinner. I'm guessing a reaction to such a person now would be, "Why should we even listen to you? Why should we read what you write? You've figured out nothing."

And he was writing a good portion of the Bible. Yes, God loves to use unfinished misfits.

I've found this really bothers some religious people. They think it's not "living in victory." I'm not exactly sure what they mean by that. Maybe "victory" means we don't sin anymore or shouldn't be talking about it. Or maybe "victory" means we always get to win at stuff.

I don't know. But I'm pretty sure real "victory," for me, is finally getting over myself. Being humble enough to know I don't know. Actually being obedient.

And maybe "victory" includes this too: I don't have to reach conclusions on everyone and everything. I know the story isn't over at all. I only see part of reality. My desire for resolution is understandable—we're all yearning for the wedding,

> I'm pretty sure real "victory," for me, is finally getting over myself. Being humble enough to know I don't know. Actually being obedient.

the kingdom in full—but it can actually inhibit my ability to appreciate what God is currently doing.

Sure, we long for resolution, but we're not there. Not yet.

Forgive me if I ever give the impression otherwise. Jesus promises there will be a beautiful end to our story, but first, we will have troubles, He says. Anyone who says they have fully arrived spiritually is peddling an illusion.

Sometimes I think about all the things I should've done, haven't done, and can't redo.

I think about Michael or a thousand other people I've known.

I think about the school bus, and Jeffrey, and Jeffrey's brokenhearted mom.

I feel like I'm lying upstairs, and someone just left the piano bench right before the final C chord.

I'd walk down and play it if I could.

TWELVE

Blessed Are the Impostors

I'M REALLY INTO TOAST.

I can't underscore that enough. It's not like a passing thing either. It's my entire life. I can't get enough toast. I never tire of it. I have a mental list of great pieces of toast I've had over the years.

That's right, let that sink in: *I fondly remember some slices of toast individually.*

I love toast dry—no butter—and burnt. I used to eat (and I'm not exaggerating here) an entire loaf of dry, burnt toast each day before 9:00 a.m. We kept a deep freeze full of loaves, and I would grab one each morning on my way to work, where I would eat all twenty-two slices.

(Note to dieters: Don't do this.)

I'm sharing this with you so you'll understand why, when I got my first full-time radio job as a one-man news department, I brought my toaster. I had a little office in the radio station, a converted closet that I made everyone refer to as the News Command Center. I couldn't find an open outlet for my

107

toaster, so I unplugged some gray box-thing in the little room and started toasting.

I was working on my computer, writing news stories, munching on some toast, when I noticed some panic in the station. I didn't know everyone that well, and whatever was going on clearly didn't involve me, so I just kept working and making toast. I'm not terribly aware of my surroundings when I'm working on something. I'm also not terribly aware of other people when I'm not working on something.

After a while, I did notice that people were running.

They were running past my News Command Center. There goes the receptionist lady. There goes my boss. There goes the production guy.

I kept typing and munching.

Until they all descended on my office, looked at me, looked down, looked at my toaster, looked at the outlet, looked at the gray box, and lunged to plug it back in.

That's when I learned that, apparently, the gray box is some kind of uplink-thing for something that keeps the station on the air. If it's not plugged in for, let's say, twenty-one minutes, that would be twenty-one minutes that the entire station would be off the air and the tri-county area would be looking at their radios wondering where everybody went.

I studied journalism at the University of Illinois. Carolyn and I were married young, while we were still in college, and we lived in married-student housing when we were seniors.

One night we were driving home to our apartment, and

there was a massive fire. It wasn't one of the apartment buildings; it was a building a couple blocks away, part of the university's horticulture department. It was eerie, because as we drove past, there was no one around. No fire department, no police, just a very large building completely engulfed.

I had an idea: *I'll cover this story! I'll get extra credit from my professor! That's what journalists do. They cover fires.* This was a story.

So we quickly drove home, and I jumped out, ran in, grabbed a pencil, and took off on foot. I got to the fire. Sirens! Fire trucks pulled up. Police pulled up.

I didn't want to get in their way, that's for sure. So I held back to watch what they were doing. I stood behind some bushes and peered out to see the action. (Note of foreboding: Don't "peer out" at a crime scene.)

They were getting hoses off the truck and springing into action and the police were there and it was all pretty frenetic and crazy and . . . was that policeman pointing at me?

Yes, he was pointing at me. He was talking animatedly to another policeman, and he was pointing at me as I peered out from behind the bush.

I thought maybe they wanted some information about the fire, and in a way that *was* what they wanted, but I didn't expect they would be so brusque and also put me in the back of the squad car.

Anyway, the next day I was at my journalism class, and I asked Professor Landay, a grizzled, former CBS White House correspondent, if he had ever been, you know, at the scene of a crime so fast that he was actually arrested for it.

I think the answer was no, because he started laughing and

actually had to leave the room and go laugh some more in the hallway.

———————————

I'm bumbley. I know that. It's my style. It won't ever change.

You're going to think I'm lying, but I'm not. When I finished typing that last sentence, I paused in my chair, stretched my arms backward—and stabbed my hand on a cactus. I'm bleeding.

I'm in a coffee shop. It's December. I'm in Pennsylvania. *Why is there a cactus in here?*

———————————

There was a guy I went to school with named Ted Sloan. He was a big guy: athletic and handsome and all that. He was nice enough too. Ted Sloan didn't beat me up at all, not even once, and I appreciated that. He was a football star. Ted Sloan surely had no self-doubt. The girls liked Ted Sloan a lot. Ted Sloan could bench-press 310 pounds. Ted Sloan was smooth. Ted Sloan knew what Ted Sloan was doing.

Whenever I would do something dumb and embarrassing in front of people, I would think about Ted Sloan. Does this stuff *ever* happen to Ted Sloan? I don't think so.

I remember once having a headache, so I sat in the bleachers of our gym during lunch hour. Lots of people did, as we waited for sixth hour to start. I was sitting by myself, looking down, reading a book, when a basketball hit me in the head at about 600 mph.

Everybody saw it and they were laughing and it did seem random, so I tried to laugh it off. But wow, it didn't help my headache. I remember sitting there, head hurting, thinking, *This kind of thing never happens to Ted Sloan. Ted Sloan never gets randomly hit in the head with a basketball.*

If you're thinking there's some moral to this story, and Ted Sloan winds up making some pivotal, unforgettably horrific mistake in the football playoffs or something, there isn't, and he doesn't. He's doing great, as far as I know. God bless him. It's not Ted Sloan's fault he's awesome.

I think a lot of us go through life with the immature mind-set I had about people like Ted Sloan. I still struggle with it: the presumption that others aren't saddled with self-doubt, that they know exactly what they're doing. We can see our fumbles and failures vividly. We can be painfully aware of our own shortcomings, missteps, and regrets.

When you're a kid, you look at adults and think they know what they're doing, and you think how it must be nice to be so confident in your every move. We look forward to getting older. We're powerless now, but when we grow up, we'll be in control.

And then we grow up, and we don't feel so in control at all.

Some of us still feel like kids, like people can see through us as we pretend to be adults, pretend to know what we're doing.

Maybe some people do feel like they have things under control. Perhaps this chapter doesn't apply to everyone. Sometimes, when I'm walking around Manhattan, for instance, I see people dashing around and they are dressed nicely and they're on their phones saying things authoritatively. Maybe they know what they're doing.

Maybe they feel like they're in complete control. They're in New York, after all. I'm from Assumption, Illinois. They can probably tell that. Maybe they feel like they know exactly where they're going and how to get there.

Or maybe they don't. Maybe, like me and possibly you, they're afraid they'll be found out. They fear someone will call them on it: "You don't know what you're doing, and we are on to you."

It must be more common than we think, because there's a name for this: *impostor syndrome.* As the *New York Times*'s Carl Richards wrote, people who are seemingly competent, motivated, and intelligent are often afraid they'll be "found out" as phonies.

> Once I learned this thing had a name, I was curious to learn who else suffered from it. One of my favorite discoveries involved the amazing American author and poet Maya Angelou. She shared, "I have written 11 books, but each time I think, 'Uh oh, they're going to find out now. I've run a game on everybody, and they're going to find me out.'"[1]

So we're not alone.

I wonder if, in the religious world, impostor syndrome doesn't manifest itself in a particularly cruel way. We not only think we'll be "outed" as incompetent, *we feel like an impostor before God Himself,* and no amount of prayer or repentance or Bible reading will ever change that.

The writer of Hebrews seemed to sense that some of us will feel like spiritual impostors:

> Seeing then that we have a great High Priest who has passed through the heavens, Jesus the Son of God, let us hold fast our confession. For we do not have a High Priest who cannot sympathize with our weaknesses, but was in all points tempted as we are, yet without sin. Let us therefore come boldly to the throne of grace, that we may obtain mercy and find grace to help in time of need. (4:14–16 NKJV)

Please know, if you feel like you can't do this, if you never feel you can go "boldly" before God because of your spiritual impostor syndrome, I completely understand. That's me too. This is why I have to hear this early and often, this promise that I can come out of hiding, that I can actually talk to God anyway.

I need to be reminded constantly. Otherwise, I'll begin to turn away from Him, frustrated that He can't really be pleased, no matter what I do. Or I may even start to write stories in my head to explain why the things I'm ashamed of really aren't so bad. I'll retrofit my own narratives to try to deal with the shame.

I suspect many people walk away from God entirely because of their desire to avoid shame, laying the intellectual groundwork as they go. They tell themselves maybe there's no God after all. Maybe if there is one, He really doesn't care what we do or who we become.

Or maybe we just slink away in shame and try not to think about Him at all anymore.

So I'm not very good at Bible stuff. I don't read it enough. I'm not good at praying either. I don't pray enough. I'm not Mr. Evangelism. I don't emote during worship because I don't feel much, honestly.

People give me religious credit for talking about Jesus-stuff on the radio, but it's also part of my job and it puts groceries on the table.

But . . .

I keep going back to this man on a cross next to Jesus. A thief. A criminal. Someone who, no doubt, wanted to "be somebody." Someone whose story was ending in shame. Someone who had nothing—zero—to offer.

No religious résumé. No great story. Nothing.

What a loser, right? But he recognized Jesus.

And then:

"Today you will be with Me in Paradise . . ."

THIRTEEN

THIRTEEN

Blessed Are the
Introverts Who Keep Trying

SOMETIMES I LIKE TO SIT ON OUR STOOP IN FRONT of our old brick townhouse here in the core of Harrisburg, Pennsylvania. I just watch people and—get this—sometimes I also try to interact with them.

Now, I'm not good at human interaction. I know that. But I also know God loves people and wants me to love people, even if I don't understand them. So I force myself to sit down and try this. For extroverts, it's probably no big deal. To me, though, this is edgy and extreme. It's like jumping out of a plane. I'm not sure what to say. I just go out there and hope my parachute opens.

It's a high-crime area. The schools are not good, and everybody knows it. There are numerous big homes here for sale for under $30,000.

There are poor people here and some middle-class people and a lot of people with drug addictions. It's about half and half, black and white, and I love that.

Honestly, it looks almost exactly like *Sesame Street*, except we have more characters here.

People pass by and I practice saying, "How you doin'?" to them. I leave off the *g*, and I say it like a statement. And I say it real quick and low too, like "howyoudoin'."

I do this because I've closely observed humans doing that and still other humans reacting positively to them.

Some people ignore me, and that's okay, but others seem to respond positively to my "howyoudoin'." I think it sounds pretty natural by now.

There's an old guy, who sits outside in a chair, who is drunk most of the time, but he's sociable. We'll call him Gene.

People are a little scared of Gene, but not because he's violent. It's because he'll talk your ear off, in an unrelenting, stream-of-consciousness storytelling style that quickly flows from one epic story to the next.

He's uninterruptible. He actually has a genius for leaving no pauses. He's the Michael Jordan of conversational dominators: You can't stop him. You can only hope to contain him.

I think he set the Green Street All-Time Record one evening sitting on our stoop when he peppered me with two hours of stories. I didn't have to say anything. It was a nonstop, continuous mix of yesterday's and today's favorites.

I like it, because while I don't want to small talk, I do want to listen. Gene wants to talk and doesn't want to listen. Perfect. It's a symbiotic relationship that way.

He used to be a hairdresser. He says he used to live with a man he was in love with for more than twelve years until that man died.

Gene's clearly lonely and only talks about himself, and

that's okay. Every few weeks he's nursing an injury to his head. He says people beat him up at night.

Gene lies often, so we don't know what to believe. Every story Gene tells has a common theme, they all end the same, and they usually involve a wedding: "And that's when the bride told me, 'Gene, this wedding was beautiful, and your ability to do my hair saved the day.'"

In his stories, Gene is always saving the day. In his stories, Gene is always needed. The circumstances change, but someone always turns to Gene in tears to thank him for rescuing their wedding, or their marriage, or their home, or something. "And then he turned to me and said, 'Gene, we'll never be able to thank you enough, and . . .'"

When it's cold out, and he gets locked out of his place, he stops in for hot coffee. Sometimes Carolyn has hot, fresh bread or something too. I know I have a higher tolerance for quirky people than most, but my wife sometimes surprises me with her kindness. One afternoon Gene was sitting at our kitchen counter, telling us another story about saving someone's wedding, and we heard a distinct trickling sound. Maybe more than trickling.

As you now know, Gene cannot be stopped, so he just kept talking. But . . . that sound. Something was pouring onto our old wood floor under Gene's chair.

I tried to butt in with, "Gene, what exactly is—" and then I saw it. He had a large open can of Colt 45 in his coat pocket, and it was dumping directly onto the floor.

Carolyn told him not to worry about it, and she grabbed some towels, and she told him to relax, and I really liked that.

But here's where it gets weirder:

A neighbor lady told us that Gene was informing the neighborhood that I, Brant Hansen, had made a pass at him. He told them that I was "running around" on Carolyn, too, and she never knew where I was and always had to go hunt me down while I was out . . . carousing? . . . or something.

Our neighbor thought it was funny, and my wife did, too, but . . . this was awkward, especially when Gene showed up the next evening asking for a cup of coffee.

I told him sure, come on in, and could we sit and talk for a moment? Carolyn went to make the coffee, and we sat down.

"Hey, uh, Gene . . . I've been hearing some weird things from neighbors."

"Oh, really?"

"Yeah. Strange things. Carrie next door said you are telling people that I made a pass at you, and that I'm a gay person, and that Carolyn runs around trying to catch me while I'm rendezvousing with people or something."

"She said I said that?"

"Yeah, she did."

"Well, I would never say such a thing. I mean, just because I am gay doesn't mean *you* are gay. I know that," he said.

"I am glad you understand. If we're going to be friends, we can't tell lies about each other. It would be really hard to be your friend like that."

"Oh, absolutely."

"Um . . . let's get the coffee now if you want."

"Wonderful! You know, just yesterday a woman asked me if I could do her hair, so . . ."

This neighborhood is a weird and wonderful place.

Anyway, I sit on the stoop and watch people, and

occasionally people talk to me and I try to keep it going without embarrassing myself.

A few weeks ago, a guy was walking to my neighbor's house, an older gentleman who takes on a hippie persona. This guy does the hippie thing too. Probably sixty years old, bandana, tie-dye, walking barefoot on the sidewalk . . . He was embracing the whole cliché, and I kind of respect that.

He stopped and introduced himself. He even asked me what I do for a living. I told him I do radio and I write and stuff, but my main reason for being in Harrisburg was to work with CURE International at their support center.

"What's that?"

Now *this* I can talk about. This is going to be easy. "CURE is a hospital network. We do surgeries for kids in developing countries—kids who have correctible disabilities. We heal kids with clubfoot or hydrocephalus, and stuff like that, and we tell them God loves them."

That made him mad.

"Well, that makes me mad."

"I don't understand that. Why? I'm genuinely curious."

"Because it's a Christian thing, right? You tell people God loves them, and then do something like that. And then they'll wind up being Christians."

"Well," I said, sitting on my stoop, "we let them know why we're doing it, but we don't coerce anyone at all, and we heal anyone regardless of their beliefs, obviously."

"Doesn't matter. When someone is healed like that, or sees their kid healed like that, they're going to be convinced. And I hate religion, because it's nothing but destructive. So I oppose this. Nothing personal."

He was actually saying this in a nice, matter-of-fact way. I wasn't insulted or anything, just interested.

"Okay, you're saying religion is destructive, but the founder of my religion told us to heal the sick. So these kids go from a life of sitting on a mat, begging, to getting to go to school. And they get to avoid physical pain and abuse, and get to run and play with their friends. How is that destructive?"

"All the problems in the world are created by religion, so making more of it is bad. We need peace, and that can only happen if we get rid of the idea of God and religious people."

I told him violence and wars are a human thing, not just a religious-people thing, and we need only look at the performance of atheistic regimes of the last one hundred years or so to see as much.

He didn't agree with that. But he was actually a nice guy. He just said what he thought. I think what he thinks is wrong.

I've asked God to help me love humans, and now I watch them from my stoop. Years ago I only wanted to live in the country, far away from anyone. I wanted to be removed from people. Too much hassle.

I once heard Timothy Keller say that God loves cities more than the country, because He loves people more than He loves trees. That challenged me, so I didn't like it, but it's hard to argue.

So here we are. It's just that the problem with being around broken people is, you know, all the broken people.

We have these two dogs, Nigel (named after the guy from *Spinal Tap*) and Arwen (from *Lord of the Rings*). They've got problems. Nigel is missing a leg, for starters, and Arwen looks like a mash-up, not of dog breeds, but of entirely different, unrelated species: part Chihuahua, yes, but also part squirrel, and maybe there's a bat in there somewhere. Neither dog has been invited to the Westminster Dog Show.

Anyway, Carolyn was out walking them on our street a few months ago, in broad daylight, and a guy attacked her. He first came up our street and threw a hammer at her, and when he missed, he decided to charge her and grab her.

He put her in a headlock, threw her around, and tossed her on the street before finally taking off.

She called the police and called me in tears, and I instantly regretted living here.

She was okay physically, thank God. But we were perplexed by the lack of police response. They didn't do anything to the guy. We gave them a description, his address, everything— even photos, which weren't hard to get because he continued to walk by our home every day.

Carolyn would be reading or knitting or something, and right outside our window, there he was again. Hammer Guy.

I called the police and the mayor's office and couldn't understand why no action was being taken. I wondered if I should do something myself, but couldn't imagine that having a positive outcome.

Nothing I was doing was making any difference.

Finally, I decided I'd go to City Hall, wherever that was, and start . . . doing . . . something. I didn't know what. But I'd go downtown and make someone, in some office somewhere, explain to me why this guy wasn't being arrested.

I walked around and went in several very nice, but also

wrong, buildings. Finally, I walked in a front door, and—no lie—in the lobby there was a big news conference going on. It was about crime. The chief of police and the mayor were there. They asked, "Does anyone have any questions?"

So I thought maybe I should go ahead and ask . . .

The headline the next day: "Local Man Crashes Press Conference."

I didn't mean to crash anything. It was all very calm. I just heard them ask for questions, and I had some earnest questions. One was, "Why won't you arrest the guy who attacked my wife?"

That did it. The guy was arrested.

He's out on bail now. We see him occasionally. He's a young guy, early twenties, and he clearly is struggling with a mental disability. We want the judicial process to do its thing, but we're actually praying he can get the help he needs.

People thought we were nuts to move into this neighborhood, and maybe we were, but even after this, my wife is still thankful we did.

I guess this place could drive an introvert crazy. But it's weird how even my heart can soften toward someone, or some-*where*, if I think about people and pray for them over time.

I've been learning about this:

> "Teacher, which is the great commandment in the law?"
>
> Jesus said to him, "'You shall love the LORD your God with all your heart, with all your soul, and with all your mind.' This is the first and great commandment. And the second is like it: 'You shall love your neighbor as yourself.'"
> (Matt. 22:36–39 NKJV)

While it's common to believe we need to learn to love ourselves before we can love others, Jesus seems to take our self-love for granted. We already look after ourselves, root for ourselves, feed ourselves, take ourselves to the bathroom, even pray for ourselves whenever we're in trouble. That's real commitment. And it all comes pretty easily, actually.

What He does not take for granted is that we love God and others. While it's certainly fashionable to agree with the "love others" part, I'm convinced I can't really do that without obeying the first part—loving God.

Sure, I can love people who stroke my ego in some way (even if it's just to tell myself, "Look how I love these tough-to-take people!"). But to truly love my neighbor as I do myself? I can't skip the first part. Love for people who offer nothing or who only hurt you? That's supernatural.

I'm also learning that people don't suspect that God can find them lovable. It's my job to prove to them that He does.

So my wife just walked in the door as I was typing this chapter. She told me the lady next door just surprised her by handing her a big rock.

The big rock had a fresh painting of Jesus' mother, Mary, on it. The lady next door just painted it.

"I painted this for you guys. You can put it in the flower patch," she told Carolyn. We have a tiny flower patch next to the curb. So she put it there and went back inside.

Then a guy walked up the sidewalk, looked at it, and promptly spat on it. Repeatedly.

That was five minutes ago. I think I mentioned this place is interesting.

We moved here from Rocklin, in northern California, which is as suburban as suburbia can get. Every home was large and neat as a pin. People took their grass very, very seriously.

(The older lady across the street was an absolute marvel. Not kidding: I once saw a leaf slowly wafting to the ground in their immaculate, deep-green front yard. Then the front door opened. She came out, picked up that leaf, and went back inside. I admire that kind of vigilance.)

I sort of got to know one outgoing family nearby. They were nerdy and I liked that. Friends! But they found an even bigger house in another part of town so they moved away.

One spring I visited my friend Seth, who lives in Manhattan on the Upper West Side. He has a wife and three little kids, and they're crammed, by suburban standards, into one of those New York apartments.

When he first took me to his building to show me where they live, we got in a tiny elevator and started going up. Another guy got on the elevator with us. I asked Seth, "So, do you know your neighbors here?"

He turned to the other guy.

"Dave, do we know our neighbors here?"

The guy on the elevator, now known to me as Dave, laughed and said, "We don't have much choice. We're kinda crammed in here!"

I like that. Isn't that odd? I'm an introvert, and I like that.

I'm small-town born and raised. I have robotic social skills. I hate being interrupted. I'm awkward. I'm self-conscious.

But I realize now I'm here (in Harrisburg, and on planet Earth) to love people, one way or the other. It might feel like daredevilry to do it, but I'm going to keep trying.

I know I need other humans too.

I asked God to change my heart. Somewhere along the way, He apparently decided He'd do that. Slowly, yes, but He's doing it.

Living near people—people you can't avoid!—can be a very good thing.

God loves them more than trees, I've heard.

FOURTEEN

Blessed Are the Perpetual Strugglers

WE ONCE HAD A COCKATIEL NAMED MEEKO. WHEN we found him outside in a tree, we asked around, and though he was clearly someone's pet, no one would claim him. We knew we couldn't just set him free, so we took him in.

He was a good bird. He said stuff like, "Pretty bird!" and he scratched around in his cage and we loved watching him. He loved to be let out, so he'd anxiously wait for us to open his little door, and he'd sit on the kids' shoulders, and he was a fantastic little bird-friend.

One day Meeko saw an egg. But it wasn't really an egg; it was an egg-shaped shaker: a little percussion instrument. It was egg-sized and egg-shaped, yes, but it was also green and had the logo for the local music store on it.

Anyway, Meeko desperately wanted to be with it. When we let him out, he'd flutter straight to the egg. We got a kick out of it, so we let him do it.

His devotion to the fake egg got to the point that he'd raise a ruckus from inside his cage until he could be with the egg.

127

To quiet him, we put it in his cage, and he'd stand next to it, silently. No more shrieking.

No more anything, actually. Now, amazingly, when we opened his cage door, he didn't want to come out. He didn't want to flutter about freely, didn't want to entertain the family. He stopped saying things. It was all about the egg. It was pretty funny.

Until it wasn't.

He clearly attached immense significance to it. We realized he was waiting for the egg to hatch. He thought it meant family or something. I don't know. I'm not a bird expert.

But it went from being amusing to kind of sad. Meeko wanted the fake egg, and only the fake egg, and it was never going to hatch.

Meeko's heart and soul, the focus of all his desires, was plastic, and it wasn't ever going to change.

Ultimately, we took the egg from him. He didn't like it, but I think he would have willingly spent the rest of his life protecting a baby bird that would never exist.

I think about Meeko sometimes, and about us. I think about the things I find addictive, and how they're always based on a substitute: a cheap imitation of something that's genuinely real and good.

I suspect God gives us drives to do things, to be things, to develop our gifts. Rightly applied, all those things wind up being a blessing to people. They help us flourish and help others flourish too.

Blessed Are the Perpetual Strugglers

But we get offered substitutes. Things that feel like the real thing. Things that give us the emotional or neurological pay-off, but with a shortcut.

Honestly, I think those of us who find relating to humans to be challenging and draining are in particular danger here. I suspect we're more likely to opt out and settle for the less-than-real. It's less awkward. It's less risk. And it certainly means less struggle.

But that's just it: we *have* to struggle. It's striking how often people think that a longstanding, ongoing struggle against a particular temptation means they are somehow failing.

No. You're not failing. *The struggle means God is still working in you.* Do not stop struggling. We should expect struggle as part of the Christian life. Before His crucifixion, we know that Jesus Himself struggled with what He knew God wanted Him to do (Matthew 26). Paul wrote extensively about his own continuing struggles against his own desires. He'd struggle, fail, and struggle again.

We're supposed to do the same. We may become discouraged, but we keep going. We try again. Why? *Because the ongoing effort itself honors a God who loves us.*

> The struggle means God is still working in you.

Setbacks need not be permanent. They need not define us. A friend of mine, Sy Rogers, told me it's like riding a bike on a long trip. You might be doing well, go two hundred miles, and then crash into a ditch. You don't say, "Oh no, now I have to go back and start all over."

129

You get back up, and get on the bike, and start pedaling. Those two hundred miles were real.

We've been taught in many ways that struggling is a bad thing, that "success" is all that matters. But it's through struggle that we learn, that we get stronger, and that we change. I'm less concerned for friends who are struggling than friends who aren't.

I don't want to take the path of least resistance. This is because that easy path means living in my own head, avoiding people, and choosing substitutes over a life of the real thing.

Our culture of pornography is an obvious example of how evil works. It's surely easier to "relate" to a virtual woman than a real one. A real, flesh-and-blood woman wants her man to take responsibility for himself. This includes, but is not limited to, being kind when he doesn't feel like it; communicating when he doesn't want to; relating to in-laws; changing diapers; and being willing to grow old together.

Virtual women, to my knowledge, do not require these things. They demand no struggle.

Evil is a shortcut. A fake. Always.

Another example: Video games give me a little adrenaline boost, a little jolt of adventurous heroism without doing anything actually adventurous or heroic. No one benefits.

I don't think gaming is evil, but I sure don't want to look back on my life at age seventy-five and realize that so many of my "adventures" were unreal. I won't be able to bear the thought that my thirst to accomplish, and my hunger to relate, were sated by the equivalent of Meeko's green egg.

Real humans can be heartbreaking, God knows. But I don't want to settle and give up the struggle so easily.

Real-world evil doesn't dress itself up with a creepy hockey mask or like a member of KISS. Real-world evil can even be a seemingly good thing . . . that crowds out the real thing.

It might seem "private," but it never is.

I know this because when I give in, when I cease the struggle, I'm not the man I should be. I'm actually grouchier. I'm less patient. I'm less joyful. I'm less loving. I'm less grateful. I'm less peaceful too. I think of others less, and have less energy for them. Oddly, in this way, giving up our struggles and giving into ourselves makes our lives heavier, not lighter.

My hidden behaviors affect others because the behaviors keep me from being who I need to be for my family, my neighbors, my coworkers, or even my enemies.

"Private" is a myth. Maybe nobody saw me drop the stone in the pond, but they can sure see the ripples.

———

I think one of the real catch-22s of being an introvert is that we want to be alone . . . until we don't.

We resist being placed in situations where we're forced to regularly interact. We don't want to be penned in. We're always leaning toward the door, metaphorically and even literally.

We certainly don't want to commit to being in a regular setting where we feel like we can't get out.

This is probably why I'm obsessed with escape scenarios. (In my mind, I routinely rehearse scenarios where I'm suddenly trapped by robots or aliens or a rabid elk, and now what do I do?! And then give myself fifteen seconds to come up with a plan. Maybe everybody does this? No?)

The local YMCA is offering a two-hour self-defense class. It started last night. It's free. I want to learn self-defense moves. Did I go to this class?

No, I did not go to this class, because I was afraid I might be trapped with people and there wouldn't be a way out. It also might be fun and interactive in a good way. But I don't know, because—you probably remember this part—I chickened out.

> **Apparently I want to escape from people so badly that I escaped from the class that teaches people how to escape from people.**

Apparently I want to escape from people so badly that I escaped from the class that teaches people how to escape from people.

When I do commit, when I do show up, I always want to hedge my bets. I want a way out.

The deepest problem with this, of course, is not just that I miss out on some potentially awesome self-defense moves.

It's that I do yearn for people. I do yearn to be known. I want to be part of a group. I see camaraderie; I see people who've gone through something together, and I watch them take a group photo, laughing at inside jokes, and I wish I was in there.

So I've learned I have to commit.

My desire—whether it's because I'm an introvert, or a modern Westerner, or a guy who tends to be lazy—is to always keep my options open. But I've found that keeping all my options open is a great way to wind up truly alone.

I've learned that the only real poetry in life comes from closing off options. Committing to people. Allowing myself to be "trapped."

I remember talking to a wise friend of mine about the church community he was part of, that my wife and I were slowly, carefully joining. We were now seeing the quirks of the leaders, the petty behavior and theological craziness of some of the members, and the difficult relationships in the community. It was messy.

He agreed with me about all the problems. I asked him how he and his wife still continued to be part of it.

"Well, we've cast our lot with these people."

Huh.

He "cast his lot" with these people. That means they were all in. Yes, there were plenty of reasons to bail, plenty of reasons to start over with new, possibly less annoying people. But . . . they had bound themselves to these people.

This sounds completely un-American, and it certainly runs counter to my nature. I like choices.

A few minutes ago, I clicked on a link that said, "Here are the 36 Top Kinds of Peanut Butter, Ranked!" Thirty-six top peanut butters. This ignores the middling and bottom peanut butters, of course. These are only the elite-of-the-elite top thirty-six. We sure like having options.

My wise friend decided just to stick with people. My MO is different. I slowly disappear, back to comfort. Back to aloneness. I've done this too many times.

Look, you can always keep your options open, but don't

expect to have any great stories to tell. Great stories always involve faithfulness, even when things are difficult and messy.

"Faithless is he that says farewell when the road darkens," said Gimli to Elrond.[1] (I tried to make it all the way through this book without quoting *LotR*, but I can't help it.)

I don't want to commit, but I have to. I want to live life as a free agent, but I also want to be a part of some great stories. I can't have it both ways.

> You can always keep your options open, but don't expect to have any great stories to tell.

I have to *decide* things, and that means cutting off options. In fact, that's what the word *decide* means: "to cut off." It's from the same root as *scissors*. It has a finality to it too. It's also the root at work in *suicide*, *homicide*, and *regicide*.

When I decided to get married, I didn't fully know what I was doing—who does?—but I did have the general impression I was cutting off other options. This included the option of not only pursuing other potential romantic interests but the option of living the single life, responsible to no one but myself.

When we got married, we committed to the struggle. (By the way, one subtle indication that marriage is going to be a challenge: it starts with you taking a vow, in front of a crowd of people, that you will not quit.)

But that's the thing about marriage: yes, I lost a tremendous amount of freedom, but I gained it too. We've been married more than twenty-five years. And still, she wants to be around me. It's breathtaking to me. It's something I wouldn't be free to experience if I hadn't cut off other options.

I'm free to have the memories of being an everyday father because I bound myself to these little people in my house. I could have pursued other things. I could have been "free" and left. But I didn't.

I'm free to remember thousands of bedtime songs and prayers and luminous eyes looking up at me and giggling at a funny turn in a story I'm making up. I lost my freedom, but I gained it too. I'm free to know what that feels like.

Marriage is just an example. The point is, there are so many things we deeply yearn for but cannot be free to experience without surrendering our freedom in the first place. If we never commit—be it to a people, or to God, or to a beautiful cause—we will miss so much that is profound.

We find freedom by losing it.

I love how Richard Foster put it: "Absolute freedom is absolute nonsense! We gain freedom in anything through commitment, discipline, and fixed habit."[2]

Commitment and discipline necessitate struggle. There's no way around this. It is not good enough for me to take the path of least resistance. If I avoid the struggle of relationship, I avoid discomfort, inevitable awkwardness, embarrassment, disillusionment, frustration, betrayal, loss, and all kinds of heartbreak. In other words, I avoid being fully human.

Adam McHugh wrote a book called *Introverts in the Church*, where he calls us out for our tendency to take the easy way and disappear into ourselves:

We can become mired in our inner worlds, to the exclusion of relationships and actions that would bring the healing and joy we seek. Our inner reflections can become excessive to the point of inaction. Introversion should never be an excuse for laziness or sin. Understanding our introversion is not the end of our self-discovery and growth; it is a beginning point for learning how to love God and others as ourselves.[3]

I'm convinced of this: anyone who succeeds in keeping all options open will wind up very alone.

Anyone who does only what comes naturally, who abandons the struggle, will wind up being less than what he or she could have been.

And, like Jesus said, anyone who loses his life for His sake . . . will find it.

FIFTEEN

Blessed Are the People
Who Do Church Anyway

SUMMING UP A BIT:

1. Humans are hypocritical. They're deceptive. They tend to be obsessed with themselves. They're not as logical as they think they are. They're often blindly judgmental. They complain. And gossip too. They are—only sometimes unwittingly—cruel. They desperately want to feel good about themselves. They're prone to addiction. And so forth and on and on.
2. I'm all that stuff too.
3. I have to love people anyway.
4. Recognizing the truth of point 2 really helps me with point 3.
5. Wow, I love making numbered lists.
6. I'm going to make another one soon in this very chapter. I think you'll like it. (I actually got excited about

using Roman numerals for this one, but my editor said she thinks it's a bad idea. See how frustrating people can be? Sheesh.)

Given that people are aggravating, and church people are people, I can expect church people to be aggravating. (That's the transitive property of equality at work right there.) God was not naïve about this, I trust, when He decided to live among us anyway.

As an introvert with a long, even brutal list of negative church experiences, it is exceedingly easy for me to decide to try to go it alone, to avoid Christian community. But I simply mustn't do this. Here's why:

1. I need Christian community because . . . my ability to justify myself is a force of nature. It's nearly unstoppable.

We're all this way. We tend not to question our motives. We don't question our desires. We want what we want, and we will reshape reality to fit it. (I wrote extensively about this in my previous book, which you should purchase multiple copies of immediately, called *Unoffendable*.)

Left in isolation, then, we will write narratives in our heads that always feature us as the Good Person or the victim. Humans are absolute masters at this.

There's a famous Bible story of David, a "man after God's own heart" (Acts 13:22), who spots an attractive young woman. He's king, so he gets what he wants, and he has lots of women. Now he wants her. He takes her. He has her husband, a loyal soldier, sent to the front to die so he can have her to himself. He does.

He justifies it all in his head. Somehow he works it out so it's all okay. It takes a crafty, wise friend to get him to actually see how inexcusable what he's done really is.

We rewrite reality to fit what we want. It takes other people, wise people who love us, to snap us out of it.

Left to myself, I will eventually justify *anything*. You will too. We need honest people around us who understand this, and who are willing to puncture our self-righteousness.

2. *I need Christian community because . . . wisdom spares me from suffering.*

I've learned that wisdom ultimately brings freedom, and foolishness brings pain. There are a lot of proverbs about this. Like this one:

> Spend time with the wise and you will become wise,
>> but the friends of fools will suffer. (Prov. 13:20 NCV)

I have to spend time with people who are humble enough to seek God's wisdom, who are growing in their understanding of the kingdom and how it actually works. I need people around me who are genuinely seeking to align themselves with what God values, rather than what the larger culture is constantly telling them to value.

My response to this in the past was simple: "Great. I need wise people. You know where I can find them? At the library. In books. I can read what they've written, and that should be enough."

Too easy.

My love of books is intense. Books are essential. They

speak across generations. They challenge my thinking. They expand my horizons. Reading is fundamental, you know. Is there anything books *can't* do . . . ?

Why, yes, as it turns out: they can't love me.

They can't call me out, after observing life in my home, and say, "Brant, you know what? You come across too harsh with your kids."

They can't tell me they saw how I handled a tough situation and they were really proud of me.

When books make me uncomfortable, I can shut them and drop them off at Goodwill. I can't really do that with humans. I've tried this.

I have to spend time with wise people—actual wise humans—and let them know me, and even let them correct me.

> When books make me uncomfortable, I can shut them and drop them off at Goodwill. I can't really do that with humans. I've tried this.

Once, when we were first married, my wife and I messed up our lease. We had to leave our apartment and found out our new one wasn't available for another three weeks. We were attending a church at the time, though we didn't really know anyone. They had a prayer request time at the end of the service. My wife stood up, told people about our mess-up, and said if anyone knew of somewhere we could go for a few weeks, please let us know.

A couple named Chris and Bridget told us we could stay in the guest room of their apartment. They'd been married five years, and he was finishing his PhD/MD program. They seemed nice enough. Chris was into *Lord of the Rings* and even made his own chain-mail armor, so I knew he was cool.

He was. But warning: after living with people in close community for a while, you get exposed.

One day Chris asked to sit down and talk to me. He told me, as kindly and directly as possible, that I needed to rethink how I was treating Carolyn. He said I wasn't kind enough with her. I was too stern and didn't demonstrate that I valued her. I needed to work on that, he said.

I felt dumb. It bugged me. I wanted to defend myself. But I got to see how Chris's marriage worked, too, and I respected it. I couldn't imagine how bringing this up benefited him. I knew he and Bridget actually loved us. I took it to heart.

That was a good move. It was a good three weeks.

We still thank God that we messed up our lease. I haven't talked to him for a few years, but I still think of Chris as one of my best friends ever. I'm thankful he shared his wisdom. I didn't even know I needed it.

Books can't do that. They can't kick my rear end.

I need people to spur me on. There's even a "one another" about that: "Spur one another on toward love and good deeds" (Heb. 10:24).

The thing about spurs: they can smart a little bit.

I have to be humble. I have to be willing to be lovingly corrected. If I'm not, I'm going to suffer.

3. I need Christian community because . . . other people show me different aspects of God.

I'm a big fan of "The Inklings," a group of British writers and thinkers who prodded one another artistically and spiritually in the 1930s and '40s at Oxford. C. S. Lewis, J. R. R. Tolkien, and Charles Williams were three of the principals. They certainly didn't agree on everything, but they enjoyed one another's company. Lewis, in particular, seemed to absorb the literary styles and ideas of the others.

When Charles died in 1945, Lewis wrote that he'd not only miss Williams, he'd miss part of Tolkien too (here referred to as "Ronald").

> In each of my friends there is something that only some other friend can fully bring out. By myself I am not large enough to call the whole man into activity; I want other lights than my own to show all his facets. Now that Charles is dead, I shall never again see Ronald's reaction to a specifically Caroline joke. Far from having more of Ronald, having him "to myself" now that Charles is away, I have less of Ronald. Hence true Friendship is the least jealous of loves. Two friends delight to be joined by a third, and three by a fourth, if only the newcomer is qualified to become a real friend. They can then say, as the blessed souls say in Dante, "Here comes one who will augment our loves."[1]

I have to believe this dynamic is at work in our understanding of God. I might grow up with a certain perception of Him that's immature and one-sided, but it changes when I get to see, up close, how others relate to Him. I read the Bible differently. I see things through their eyes too.

4. *I need Christian community because . . . I need to confess to people.*

You know how I mentioned our penchant for self-justification? And how it's *almost* unstoppable?

Confession stops it.

There are something like fifty-nine different "one anothers" in the New Testament, like the oft-repeated "love one another" (John 13:35) and "submit to one another" (Eph. 5:21) and "offer hospitality to one another without grumbling" (1 Peter 4:9).

Another is, "Confess your sins to each other" (James 5:16).

It's so difficult and so freeing. Instead of cowering in shame, or having to jump through intellectual and moral hoops to somehow justify ourselves, we just admit we're wrong. We tell someone.

We hear ourselves doing it. We are reminded of our need for humility. No more games. We expose our shame to the light of day and find that it withers.

And so often we hear those wonderful words, "Me too."

5. *Speaking of the fifty-nine "one anothers," I need Christian community because . . . I can't do any of them myself.*

Serve one another in love. Carry each other's burdens. Be patient with each other. Forgive each other. Submit to one another out of reverence for Christ. Teach one another. Encourage each other. Be kind and compassionate to one another. The list goes on and on, and none of it makes sense if I think I can do this without my spiritual brothers and sisters.

Yes, I want to avoid people or only be with a select few I find amusing, easy to be around, and who happen to affirm me and anything I want. But that requires nothing.

> **Yes, I want to avoid people or only be with a select few I find amusing, easy to be around, and who happen to affirm me and anything I want. But that requires nothing.**

None of the "one anothers" make sense in that world. If I'm going to be intellectually consistent as a believer, if I have any real desire to follow Jesus, I have to obey in this area. Otherwise, I'm just worshiping me.

6. *I need Christian community because . . . other people need me.*

I may be annoying and ask pesky questions, or make them wonder why I can't just go along with everything, but yes, they need me.

If I isolate myself, if I pull away from intentional community with Jesus-followers, I rob people of what I can bring to their lives. This sounds arrogant, but it's the same with everyone.

If you think you can bring nothing, you are mistaken. People often aren't aware of their own gifts or devalue them. If you put stock in Scripture, you have to accept that God has given you *something* to add to build up others in that context. If I isolate myself, I'm being selfish.

British theologian N. T. Wright wrote about Jesus' own vision for what "church" means:

> [Jesus] apparently envisaged that, scattered about Palestine, there would be small groups of people loyal to himself, who would get together to encourage one another, and would act as members of a family, sharing some sort of common life and, in particular, exercising mutual forgiveness.[2]

Of course, if "church" is simply an organization that offers programs and worship services, this doesn't make much sense. But if it's a *family* that encourages each other to spiritually grow, it's something wonderful. We all get to play.

7. I need Christian community because . . . I need people not to break up with.

When we lived in Florida, we were part of a "simple church." We met in homes and at the beach and in restaurants. Our group grew rapidly. There were fifty or sixty of us after a while. We got to know one another very, very well.

Once, at a Sunday gathering, a new guy invited some of the guys over for a Ping-Pong night. It was great fun.

Until it suddenly turned into a big, loud argument. It was embarrassing. I'm still not sure exactly what happened. I remember being challenged to fight. I remember passionately making my point while gesticulating with my Ping-Pong paddle. I remember being a jerk.

I'll spare you the other details. It was one of the nastier table tennis–related evenings I've been part of.

Afterward, I wanted to leave the group—it all seemed so stupid—but thought, *Where else do I go? These are my people. They're family.*

There were a lot of apologies, a lot of long conversations.

It took a while, but "Ping-Pong Night" became a reference we all laugh about. As ludicrous as the whole thing was, at the time, it seemed like a deal-breaker. I was done. I wanted to move on. I know other guys did too.

But we didn't. We knew we had to work it out, had to talk at length, no matter what. If churches are really just businesses, well, no problem. Move on. Make another consumer choice. But families don't just move on.

> If churches are really just businesses, well, no problem. Move on. Make another consumer choice. But families don't just move on.

To be sure, the great thing about a church group like that is you really get to know people. The bad thing about a church group like that is you really get to know people.

People, it turns out, tend to be wrong about a lot of things. They don't raise their kids the way you raise yours. They have different standards, artistically and morally, with regard to what they'll watch on Netflix. They make bad financial decisions. What are they thinking? They're moody. They get excited about something, then don't want to follow through.

They have some theologically sketchy ideas too. Sometimes really sketchy. The whole "other people" world out there is a big mess.

A way to avoid all this, of course, is to merely attend a church service of some sort. It'll be ordered just so, and you'll see the backs of everyone's heads as they face the stage, and you can pretend everyone has their act together. It's all under control. You're in no danger whatsoever.

So here's Hansen's Law: *It's only when you actually get to know people that you discover how weird everyone really is.*

And here's a corollary: *Yep, everybody's really weird.*

Still, Jesus designed us to be together. One reason, according to Wright, is that "Jesus' followers needed to know how to put into practice the way of forgiveness he was advocating."[3]

People will give you lots of occasions for practicing this, as you've probably noticed.

I wonder, too, if introverts in particular might be too perfectionistic about these relationships. We want it to be more than it can ever live up to being, so we're that much more disappointed.

Henri Nouwen wrote that there's a loneliness that will persist, even with the best of friends or church family:

> In community, where you have all the affection you could ever dream of, you feel that there is a place where even community cannot reach. That's a very important experience. In that loneliness, which is like a dark night of the soul, you learn that God is greater than community.[4]

And yet, there's something wonderful about not breaking up. There's something refreshing about saying, "I don't totally understand you, and we disagree about a lot of important things, and normally, we might not be friends, but we're brothers, and I'm not going anywhere."

Remarkably, Jesus Himself said this is how people will really know who He is. Look at His prayer for His followers, just before His arrest:

> I have given them the glory that you gave me, that they may be one as we are one—I in them and you in me—so that they may be brought to complete unity. Then the world will know that you sent me and have loved them even as you have loved me. (John 17:22–23)

If unity is such a big deal to Jesus, it simply makes no sense for me to call myself His follower while remaining independent.

If unity is such a big deal to Jesus, it simply makes no sense for me to call myself His follower while remaining independent.

There's an old song about how breaking up is "hard to do," but you know what's harder than breaking up? Not breaking up.

G. K. Chesterton, who was a British writer, literary critic, and philosopher, was also a champion of marriage. Even as he often waxed poetic about marriage, he knew full well how hard it could be.

> I have known many happy marriages, but never a compatible one. The whole aim of marriage is to fight through and survive the instant when incompatibility becomes unquestionable. For a man and a woman, as such, are incompatible.[5]

I think it's true beyond man/woman relationships. We're all ultimately incompatible. If I were to meet my exact clone, it would just be a matter of time before I and me would go our separate ways. We'd have some toast, quote Monty Python lines to each other, share some laughs . . . and then start getting really annoyed.

Things tend toward disorder, toward breaking down, and toward entropy and decay. Our refusal to break up, our refusal to isolate out of a desire for convenience or fear of being hurt, is evidence of life.

It's also evidence that grace is real, and it works.

Yes, Jesus-followers are an odd group. Some are hard to take. Some are annoying. Some would say the same of me. But there's something wonderful, mysterious, even shocking, about people who stay together anyway.

SIXTEEN

Blessed Are the
Melancholy and the Depressed

ONE PARTICULAR EVENING IT HIT ME ALL AT ONCE:
I've wasted my life.

All of it.

I thought back on the many days I'd lived and how I'd spent them. I'd accomplished nothing. I misused the time I had been given. I felt the total weight of the failure, the squandered opportunities.

I broke down and cried. I was alone. A woman, on hearing my sobs, came in the room and sat down next to me. I turned to her and let it all out.

"I've wasted it all. What have I ever really done? Time has gone by, and I've got nothing to show for it. I've failed. I'm a failure."

The woman next to me was very concerned for me. She was deeply saddened.

She was also alarmed, because she was my mom, and I was seven years old.

I don't remember a period of my life when the "I'm a failure" recording hasn't looped through my brain.

When I've shared about this on the radio, I get the predictable reaction from some, about how I must not be "living in victory" or must be lacking faith, and so forth. And I'd certainly love to grow in my faith.

But what about that seven-year-old?

Is it possible some of us are just given to depression or compulsive thoughts, through no fault of our own?

Is it possible that this is our lot in life, our struggle?

Is it possible that the recurring thought—*You're a failure*—will be chasing me, in some way, until I die?

And—here's a crazy-sounding question: Is it possible to struggle with depression and be *joyful* . . . at the same time?

> **Is it possible to struggle with depression and be *joyful* . . . at the same time?**

Years ago a good friend of mine, who's a doctor, suggested I try an antidepressant. I'd never seriously thought about it before.

I talked with a wise counselor about it, who also suggested it might be good for me. I had reservations. One of our conversations went like this:

Me: But what if they'd put Mozart on meds? Would he have still produced great works if they had treated him that way?

Doctor: I don't know. So . . . are you producing great
works?

Me: Nope.

Doctor: Okay, next question?

I did try it. I struggled with the idea, but I tried it. And
wow, did it make a difference.

It felt like my brain cooled off. Like I was finally able to be
present with people, without the nonstop self-incrimination.

I wasn't as viciously angry at myself as I had been my entire
conscious life.

I could even take naps—something I couldn't do before—
because I wasn't roiling with regret. Previously, I'd lie there and
think about all the ways I'd blown it on the air that morning,
or how I never should have said that awkward, dumb thing
five, ten, or twenty-five years ago. I'd think about how I was
failing as a dad, how we could only afford a small place with
no yard to play in.

It wasn't rational, of course. And it was utter self-absorption,
too, which gave me something else to feel bad about.

But now, with the pills? I could take a nap.

Ironically, that disturbed me. Here's what I wrote on my
blog at the time.

As a Christian, I'm uncomfortable with purely mechanis-
tic explanations for our behavior. Friends say, "What's the
struggle? Taking this pill is just like taking Tylenol for an
ache." No, it's not. I take this pill, and I'm *morally* better.
I'm not kidding.

Think about it: They tell addicts about "HALT." Watch

out, they say, when you're Hurt, Angry, Lonely, or Tired. That's when you'll be most apt to succumb to temptation, to be given to weakness, to engage in behavior and thoughts you know you don't want to do or entertain. Look out when you're Hurt. Angry. Lonely. Tired.

Now imagine taking a pill and, suddenly, you're *not* so hurt, or angry, or lonely, or tired. You'll be less likely to succumb to temptation. Your need to retreat into bad habits, addictions, and destructive behavior lessens dramatically. So you don't—because of a pill.

You're more patient with people. More loving. Less likely to argue. Less bitter, angry, or selfish.

That ain't Tylenol, folks. That's messing with who you are.

After about a year, the effects wore off dramatically.

I switched prescriptions, hoping to get back to what it felt like initially, but it didn't work.

Today, I still take a small dose of fluoxetine each day. I think it helps a little. I'm not sure. I also think (hope?) I've grown up a little. I've since read that many people with high-functioning autism use a small dose of an antidepressant for the same reason—to deal with the always-pursuing specter of failure.

Please, before you fault me for not attacking the forces of darkness with an all-out spiritual assault, before you write and tell me I'm not doing enough: I have asked God to take this from me.

I'm still asking.

Since I work with a medical healing ministry, I'm surrounded by talk of healing. I get to see permanent, freeing change. Kids who never walked before can now run and play.

Today I held in my hands a photo of a girl, maybe sixteen years old, covering her mouth, as if to hold in the joy, as she gazed down at her newly straightened leg.

She'd never seen her leg straight before; now it's straight . . . for good! It's beautiful.

I wish something like that could happen for me. I've asked God to help, please, to take whatever it is away from me, forever.

No, it hasn't happened. And you know what? Even in top-flight missionary hospitals, "it" doesn't always happen. There are conditions that can't be fully healed. There are moms who are hoping for a miracle, and our doctors have to explain why what they're hoping for may not happen.

I know people see psychological phenomena in a different light, but I don't think it always is. How we think and feel is, clearly, often the result of physiology. I've had friends who've abused drugs, and even though they've since become Christians, their thinking is clearly addled by their previous addictions.

The spiritual conversion may be real, but the physiological consequences remain.

It's not just drugs either. Our experiences, perhaps traumatic or long-term, influence our physiology too. It's such a complex thing. Our spiritual conversions may be real, but the physiological consequences remain.

So here we are, the messy lot of us, stuck on planet Earth.

———

In *A Beautiful Mind*, Russell Crowe stars as mathematician John Nash. We see Nash in his college years, brilliantly succeeding at math, but finding it difficult to relate to humans.

155

Nash doesn't have many relationships other than his wife, his good friend Charles, and Charles's sweet little niece, Marcee. Nash's mathematical gifts land him an appointment with MIT, before he's secretly hired by shadowy FBI Agent Parcher to use his mathematic abilities to crack Russian coded messages.

I can't write about this without including spoilers. The movie's worth watching, even if you know how it ends. But consider this your spoiler alert if you haven't seen this movie since it came out in 2001.

Nash eventually learns a devastating truth: he'd been hallucinating his friend Charles, even little Marcee, for years. And the FBI agent wasn't real either. His tireless, frenetic work to combat the Soviets was meaningless. No one, in fact, was retrieving all the data that he had been collecting and dropping off at a secret location.

He's been suffering from a mental illness his wife has been desperately trying to get him to confront, and he finally begins to understand the truth.

As the movie depicts the years ahead, Nash still suffers from his delusions, but he learns to live with them. He clings to the truth: they aren't real. He and his wife, Alicia, manage to survive as a couple, and Nash goes on to succeed on a spectacular level in his career, winning a Nobel Prize for his work on game theory.

On their way out of the Nobel ceremony, Nash sees Charles, Marcee, and Agent Parcher, waiting for him, smiling. Alicia asks him, "What's wrong?"

Nash says, "Nothing." And they keep walking.

And that is how I can write this book, or do much of anything, for that matter.

Brant, you're a failure! may be stuck in my head, looping

for the rest of my life. Maybe it will never, ever go away. But it's not true. I know it.

Like Alicia Nash, my wife tells me so.

And if I believe the things Jesus said—really *believe* the things He's on record saying, not just pledge allegiance to a modernized Jesus of my own devising—I have to believe God loves me and finds me very valuable. If I believe what Jesus said, I also have to believe there's an Enemy who is, above all things, a liar (John 8:44).

(To be sure, people struggle to believe in a real Evil like this: a spiritual entity who wants to destroy us in rebellion against the Creator. While the rest of humanity seems to have little trouble believing such a thing exists, we modern Westerners find such a belief too simplistic, too dated. Jesus, however, sides with the rest of the world.)

So there's the truth, and then there are the lies we believe about ourselves, things that have perhaps rattled around our brains since childhood, or other lies about ourselves pushed on us by our surrounding culture.

To be like Nash, then, from *A Beautiful Mind*, means I acknowledge the lie (*Who cares what you think, Brant? Stop writing*) and confront it repeatedly with the truth: some people *do* care. My writing can actually be a blessing to people. It can be freeing. I've seen God use it before. Yes, I'm flawed and perpetually full of self-doubt, *but I'm going to keep going.*

So my inner monologue says I'm a waste of time? I'm a failure? God is condemning me? He's turned His back on me?

So what? My inner monologue is wrong.

There's a scripture that means a lot to me now. It's in Paul's letter to the Philippians, when he says this:

And now, dear brothers and sisters, one final thing. Fix your thoughts on what is true, and honorable, and right, and pure, and lovely, and admirable. Think about things that are excellent and worthy of praise. (4:8 NLT)

I've seen this scripture reduced to a mere "power of positive thinking" reference. But notice the first word in the list: *true*.

True things. I have to fix my mind on what's true. Yes, we suffer delusions, sometimes of grandeur or failure or, commonly, both. So we're told to return to what is *true*.

This means stepping outside of myself often enough to criticize my own thoughts. I'm certainly critical of others' ideas, so why not my own? Why can't I investigate my own manners of thinking, my own seemingly logical conclusions, and ask tough questions?

This isn't double-mindedness. This is mental health.

My inner monologue simply can't be trusted. It has to be held up and cross-examined in the light of the truth.

G. K. Chesterton made the point unforgettably in *Orthodoxy*, when he wrote about those who are completely convinced of their own tight logical systems, the ones who've made all the connections, who've figured it all out: "The men who really believe in themselves are all in lunatic asylums."[1]

It's curious how our self-perceptions can vacillate even during the course of a single day. One minute we're saying, "I'm such an idiot!" for locking our keys in the car again. Then we painfully remember the selfish thing we said that hurt someone, something we can't get back.

But mere moments later, we're quietly confident we can find our own meaning in life and be our own ultimate authority.

Maybe we should question this.

I have to question, too, my own melancholy, my own depression. The writer of Psalm 42 did the very same thing:

> Why are you cast down, O my soul,
>   and why are you in turmoil within me?
> Hope in God; for I shall again praise him,
>   my salvation and my God.
>
> My soul is cast down within me;
>   *therefore I remember you.* (vv. 5–6 ESV, emphasis added)

He's acknowledging the reality of his feelings, but also the greater reality, and he's redoubling his efforts to live in view of it. His emotions simply do not square with what he knows to be true.

It's a recurring theme:

> I have to question, too, my own melancholy, my own depression.

> Why am I discouraged?
>   Why is my heart so sad?
> I will put my hope in God!
>   I will praise him again—
>   my Savior and my God! (Ps. 42:11 NLT)

We see the same pattern from the writer of Lamentations:

> My soul continually remembers [my affliction and my
> wanderings]
>   and is bowed down within me.
> *But this I call to mind,*
>   *and therefore I have hope:*
>
> The steadfast love of the LORD never ceases;
>   his mercies never come to an end;
> they are new every morning;
>   great is your faithfulness.
> "The LORD is my portion," says my soul,
>   "therefore I will hope in him." (3:20–24 ESV, emphasis
> added)

Now, if you look closely at this, it's doubly instructive: The writer doesn't say his issues are gone. He doesn't say the struggle is over. Like Nash, his "friends" are still there. And yet . . . he has hope, because of the truth.

The truth is full of God's faithfulness and mercy.

Very few people can understand this. I know this, because I've tried to explain it to people. How can someone be simultaneously struggling with depression yet be deeply joyful?

My downcast soul is rooted in my experiences, my fallenness, my physiology, my humanness. Those things are real.

But so is my joy, because it is rooted in very real hope.

I can hear the question: "Brant, are you seriously saying you can be depressed and joyful at the same time?"

Yes, that's precisely what I'm saying, which is why I'm about to write one more quick chapter about this.

SEVENTEEN

Blessed Are Those Who Don't Take Themselves So Seriously

MAYBE YOU'VE MET SOMEBODY LIKE THIS: THEY routinely tell you how depressed they are, and when you humbly remind them of some good things that are happening, they actually don't want to hear it.

Maybe you've been that way. I'm afraid I have.

"Feelings are great liars," Eugene Peterson wrote. "We think if we don't *feel* something there can be no authenticity in *doing* it. But the wisdom of God says something different: that we can *act* ourselves into a new way of feeling much quicker than we can *feel* ourselves into a new way of acting."[1]

It's odd how apt I am to hold others' feelings under a critical lens but seek to validate my own. I shouldn't indulge my desire to continually defend my depression. Yes, I should recognize it. It's real. But there are some things I've learned I can do—things I *have* to do.

1. *Remind myself of what's true.*

(We discussed this in the last chapter.)

2. *Proactively love people.*

This is not a complex thing. Like Peterson said, we can often act our way into a new way of feeling.

I've found I have to be intentional about this. I have to serve someone, somehow. Now.

If we believe that Jesus is the smartest man who ever lived, knows us through and through, and He's on our side, the "greatest command" speaks to how you and I can flourish: "'Love the Lord your God with all your heart and with all your soul and with all your mind.' This is the first and greatest commandment. And the second is like it: 'Love your neighbor as yourself'" (Matt. 22:37–39).

Somehow I've got to get out of my own head, out of myself and all my myriad narratives about Brant Hansen.

One thing that works, and it's something I can do even while alone in the car: I can pray for my enemies. Jesus told us to do it. Difficulty level: 10.

3. *Remember a fundamental, life-changing truth: I'm really, seriously not the center of the universe.*

Ever read the side of the cereal box?

I did. My brother and I used to argue over who got to read the box while we were eating the Sugar Smacks or whatever. We were able to talk our mom into buying it because it was good for us. It was fortified with—get this—*eight* essential minerals! That's a lot of minerals, Mom.

I used to think that was funny, because it almost sounded like we were eating rocks.

Until, at age thirty-two, I realized that *we are actually eating rocks.*

The zinc they talked to you about in geology? Yeah, that's the zinc in Cinnamon Toast Crunch. We're eating particles of ground dust.

Even more shocking, for those who haven't thought about it: we eat bits of ground dust because that's what we're made of—ground dust. We have to replenish the dust we're losing with some more dust.

We each lose more than fifty billion cells a day, and we've got to replace them with something, so that's where Cap'n Crunch steps in for duty. (By the way, when someone accuses you of lounging around, remind them that you're busy: "I'm replacing fifty billion cells right now. I'm tired.") You need rock bits to replace those other bits, so Kellogg's kindly sprays them on your flakes or whatever.

We're walking piles of dust. Conscious, beautiful, imaginative, emotional, self-aware . . . dust.

And we're not even the same continuous piles of dust, since we keep losing particles and exchanging them with other particles from the universe.

> We're walking piles of dust. Conscious, beautiful, imaginative, emotional, self-aware . . . dust.

This shouldn't have been a shock, since they told me in church that God made Adam out of dust. I guess I just thought maybe that was only Adam, and not me or you. It turns out that the Hebrew word *adama* means "earth." There's no elaborate naming ceremony for Adam in Genesis either. Here's the first time Adam is referred to in Genesis:

> Out of the ground the LORD God formed every beast of the field and every bird of the air, and brought them to Adam to see what he would call them. (Gen. 2:19 NKJV)

It's like calling someone "Dirt-Man" or "Ground-Boy." And that's the first reference we get to him: *So God brought the animals to Dirt-Boy to see what he would call them . . .*

And that's us. We're dust. You're "Ground-Boy," too, unless you're a girl, and even though "Eve" is a pretty classy name, you need Lucky Charms as much as we do.

That's reality. We are dust, and our lives go by in a cosmic flash. Our illusion of control can be obliterated in an instant. It might be shattered by a single sentence from a doctor in a cold exam room, a late-night phone call from a police officer, or a breaking news story on CNN.

Rich Mullins once wrote a song called "We're Not as Strong as We Think We Are." He was right.

We're frail things, made of dust, and to dust we return. Some philosophers would find this depressing. I find it breathtaking. The difference? I believe God loves us.

There is ample reason to be humble. There's certainly reason to suspect that our whole blustering, self-confident culture is playing pretend.

There's good reason to feel like this, like we don't quite know what we're doing, like we're not fully in control. Like we're not the center of the universe. Like a child.

Jesus told us to approach God this way.

In fact, He made it clear: we either approach Him this way, or we can't approach Him at all.

4. Be enormously grateful.

It's very difficult for me to be deeply depressed and grateful at the same time.

Be grateful all the time, for anything and everything. For family. For laughs. For music. For the freedom to repeatedly and unashamedly use sentence fragments.

For the fact that God would so love us, walking piles of dust that we are, and would even want to be with us forever.

> **It's very difficult for me to be deeply depressed and grateful at the same time.**

5. Be attentive to how God uses weakness. It's just how He operates.

There's something Jesus said about weakness that I simply couldn't understand.

They brought a blind man to Him and tried to trap Him in a public questioning. "Whose fault is this?" they asked.

As Jesus was walking along, he saw a man who had been blind from birth. "Rabbi," his disciples asked him, "why was this man born blind? Was it because of his own sins or his parents' sins?"

"It was not because of his sins or his parents' sins," Jesus answered. "This happened so the power of God could be seen in him." (John 9:1–3 NLT)

I bring this up because this scripture baffled me. He's blind so that the power of God could be seen in him? What? Maybe you understood it at first reading. I didn't get it.

That is, until I talked to a woman who'd just won the Teacher of the Year award for the state we were in. It was a big deal, I guess, and she apparently was a listener to my show, so it seemed like an easy interview. Her job was as a music teacher, but on her own initiative, she formed an extracurricular choir. It was a large group of students, all with a variety of significant special needs.

"Some can't sing, because they can't speak," she told me. "Others can only say the words. Some can shake a percussion instrument. Some of the kids just want to be part of it, and they can sit or stand with us. That's what they can do. And we love that."

She told me she was inspired by a scripture—the one I just referred to—about Jesus and the blind man. She said it's apparent when the choir performs, that *their very weaknesses are what glorify God.*

I asked my boss if we could have this choir be the opening act at a concert we had coming up in a few weeks. He agreed, and so did the headlining artist.

I think there were eight thousand people there. The choir took the stage wearing matching shirts, and they sang a song called "Fingerprints of God."[2] A few of the kids had solo parts; others clapped or just stood and smiled or did whatever they could. They sang about how God created us and that He's a master artist.

I'm old enough to have seen U2 on the first *The Joshua Tree* tour, and that had some great moments. But this was better.

There was something oddly freeing about it. I don't know how else to put it. Our entire culture seems designed to make people feel ashamed of themselves for falling short of the ideal of impossibly sexy, rich, or powerful. But this group, on this stage, singing that song . . . unforgettable.

I almost felt sorry for the headlining band. All they could do was show off their talent.

Jesus met a man who was born blind. And when they asked Him why the man was blind, He said it was so that God could be glorified. I think I am beginning to understand it now.

Just being honest here: I know I'm not the best writer. But I'm hoping something like what happened in that concert happens when you read this book. You may forget the author, but I hope you walk away thinking, *Oh, my God, You can use even me.*

6. See the inherent silliness in everything. And embrace it.

"Silly" gets a bad rap.

Silliness is considered a vice by most, but in fact, it's the most underrated of virtues. Today to be silly means to be "inappropriate," "absurd," or "foolish." In religious circles, you learn early on that silliness is not spiritual. When we're "spiritual," we're solemn.

We must look serious and, above all, take ourselves very seriously.

Oh, religious folk can joke, sure. But we know that when it's time to get spiritual, well, the jokes are over. Settle down.

Quietly feeling guilty? That's spiritual.

Quietly thinking of something innocently funny? No.

Crying can be spiritual.

Giggling? No.

I don't know when it happened. I'm no church historian. But clearly there was some kind of Fancy Council at Wherever when leaders got together and issued a decree or edict or something and it was clear:

"From now on, being 'spiritual' means being really solemn. So everybody start taking yourselves way-seriously, and when it's time to do God-themed stuff, everybody sit down and shut up. Or you can stand up and shut up. Okay, sit down and *then* stand up, but definitely get super-serious.

"And also: shut up."

And they very seriously voted on it, and lo, it was passed, and they walked out quietly, wearing silly hats the whole time.

Originally, *silly* had a very different meaning. It meant "innocent" and "happy." It meant "childlike" in the best way.

I just talked to a friend who's frustrated with his seven-year-old daughter. He said, "All she cares about is the next funny thing." I sympathize. I know that can be very frustrating as a parent. But I'm also thinking, *I actually love those kinds of people.*

Silly people. People who can't stop laughing, even—especially—when they're not supposed to be laughing. People who are thinking about the next funny thing. People who try to stifle laughter while they're in class or in church but they can't and you can see their shoulders shaking.

If you are like this, please hear me: I think we're actually on to something, because everything, at a very deep level, is pretty funny. I'm convinced even "heavy" people like me find a kind of lightness when we see clearly.

I'm not the only one to think so either. Karl Barth wrote that laughter is "the closest thing to the grace of God."[3]

But we're told it's not. We're told, in a thousand different ways, to take things more seriously, especially ourselves. We make serious-taking synonymous with being a real adult.

Yes, those of us who are grown up should not aspire to be child*ish*. We should take responsibility, not just for ourselves, but for others too. Yes, there's a time to understand the weight of our sin, in order to feel the lifting of it from our shoulders. Yes, there's a time for mournful solemnity, and in those times we should truly mourn. (But surely it's not every Sunday morning, is it?)

Yes to all that.

Like C. S. Lewis said, "Joy is the serious business of Heaven."[4]

G. K. Chesterton said, "The secret of life lies in laughter and humility."[5]

Indeed, it does.

Another noted social critic, Bob Dylan, said he thinks heaven will be "echoes of laughter."[6] At least that's what we think he was saying.

I'm merely saying Jesus-followers should be sillier than everyone else. We should set the pace for silly, out-sillying the world. Even those of us who struggle with depression can be good at it. Why?

We're already aware how this is going to end.

Maybe, if you're a sports fan, you've watched a big game

after it was played. You had to work or something, so you recorded the game and watched it even after you heard the good news: your team got a last-second win!

Jesus-followers should be sillier than everyone else.

It's tough to watch your team get behind by three touchdowns early on. But it's not as frustrating when you know there's going to be a comeback. You know the good guys pull it out in the end.

Much of the excitement remains—you can't wait to see the final play that wins it—but the anxiety is gone. The individual plays—the missed blocks, the dropped passes—don't bother you so much. Why should they? Maybe your clumsy team fumbles over and over. Maybe things look bleak, but you don't need to worry.

You can be lighthearted. You can maybe even laugh at the setbacks. You can hear your inner voice telling you many things. Many lies. And you can put them in their place.

Because you know how this ends.

EIGHTEEN

Blessed Are the Skeptics and Those Who Don't Know Where Else to Go

ONCE, JESUS WAS SAYING THINGS TO A CROWD OF His followers, things that were really hard to understand. I'm not sure anyone understood Him. What He was saying was confusing and disturbing.

So they deserted Him.

Jesus asked the very few that stayed behind: "You do not want to leave too, do you?" (John 6:67).

They hadn't understood what He was talking about either, of course.

But Peter, who had a habit of bluntness, did it again. He spoke up.

"Lord, to whom shall we go?" (John 6:68).

Exactly.

As I've struggled with my own doubts and, frankly, my own desire to rebel against the dishonest church culture I've been exposed to, I've had to consider the alternatives. *Where else do I go?*

I'm not writing this chapter to convert atheists. I'm writing it to people like me, who so struggle with what they've been through that they've contemplated walking away.

If I did walk away, maybe I'd be sending a message: I'm tired of the hypocrisy. I'm tired of the way people exploit others using Christianity as a guise. I'm tired of the way high-profile religious people keep advancing their own kingdoms at all costs.

And yet, if I don't go to Jesus . . . ?

He's the one who called people out for those very things. Jesus is the only one I know who both (1) acknowledges the reality of sin and then (2) actually does something about it.

I find that everyone believes in sin, by the way, even if they don't like to use the word. Everyone, including atheists, find some things morally repugnant and destructive. Richard Dawkins, a British scientist and perhaps the world's most famous atheist, has a long list of things Muslims do, for instance, that he says are simply wrong.

He says it's not a mere difference of opinion. Dawkins claims he's right, and they're wrong. He won't tell us what transcendent authority there is for this, because he doesn't think he needs one. He's a biologist, and he knows. Thus saith him.

As a skeptic, this does not work for me. If there is no purpose for this universe, there is no purpose for any of us. That's the cold, hard truth. We can pretend otherwise, but we remain mere specks of dust, floating on a pale-blue dot, and why does it matter what those specks think? So one speck's brain is telling it to be horrified by the way other specks' brains work? Really?

So what?

As I've pondered walking away from God, I've stared into the infinite "So what?" When I see atheists like Dawkins trying to contrive moral codes they use to judge others, I'm jarred by the inconsistency.

"The universe we observe has precisely the properties we should expect

> If there is no purpose for this universe, there is no purpose for any of us. That's the cold, hard truth.

if there is, at bottom, no design, no purpose, no evil and no good, nothing but blind, pitiless indifference," he wrote.[1]

And then he's as full of *oughts* and *shoulds* and *ought nots* and *should nots* as any finger-waving Sunday school teacher.

Author Larry Taunton asked him directly about this. Where does he get his standards he applies to others? "How are we to determine who's right? If we do not acknowledge some sort of external [standard], what is to prevent us from saying that the Muslim [extremists] aren't right?" Dawkins's response is . . . well, not satisfying:

> "Yes, absolutely fascinating." His response was immediate. "What's to prevent us from saying Hitler wasn't right? I mean, that is a genuinely difficult question. But whatever [defines morality], it's not the Bible. If it was, we'd be stoning people for breaking the Sabbath."[2]

So Dawkins has moral expectations he'd like others to observe, and while he has no idea where his authority comes from, he certainly knows it's not from the Bible.

Okay.

You'll notice, in his writings, that for a man who does not believe in evil or good, he rather freely uses words like *evil* and *good*. Honestly, as a skeptic myself, this is why I get the distinct impression most atheists don't really believe what they're saying.

If I walked away from God, could I walk to this and be intellectually satisfied? I'm not sure Dawkins even believes himself.

Atheist Sam Harris, for his part, resorts to the idea that free will itself is an illusion. None of us, murderers and martyrs included, really ever chooses a thing. Yet he's still a moralist who believes in absolutes.

> Indeed, religion allows people to imagine that their concerns are moral when they are highly immoral—that is, when pressing these concerns inflicts unnecessary and appalling suffering on innocent human beings. This explains why Christians like yourself expend more "moral" energy opposing abortion than fighting genocide. It explains why you are more concerned about human embryos than about the lifesaving promise of stem-cell research. And it explains why you can preach against condom use in sub-Saharan Africa while millions die from AIDS there each year.[3]

As a skeptic, I wonder why the chemicals in Harris's brain apparently prompt him to try to induce the chemicals in my brain to make me act like something Harris's brain matter would consider a better moral person. Good luck diagramming that last sentence.

Perhaps, if I walk away from faith, I can subscribe to the view of luminaries like Neil deGrasse Tyson or Elon Musk, who believe we're all very likely part of a computer simulation.[4]

I don't find this convincing either, for numerous reasons I won't bore you with. I will say it's odd, after years of being told there is no evidence for an outside designer, that we're now to believe we're all in a computer sim . . . that has a designer.

This seems ironic.

If I walk away from faith in God, I could tell myself, perhaps, that belief in God is really the root of humanity's problems. It's the reason for war. It's the reason for oppression.

But then I'm confronted with the history of the last century, and it becomes obvious—after one hundred million innocent deaths at the hands of their own atheist governments[5]—that atrocities are the result of human selfishness, and we humans will use whatever means at our disposal to our own ends, be it "God" or government, or both.

We just like having a means to power and control. If religion offers power, of course selfish people will use it. Maybe this is why, as I understand it, Jesus replaced religious power structures with Himself.

There was to be no gain, no glamour, no rush of power in the church. He's the head of the church; we're all on one level. *Leadership* meant servantship, period. No power games.

But we humans will use whatever we can, and if Christianity, or anything else, can be reshaped into a spotlight, a place on stage, or power over the masses, you can expect people will reshape it.

I could blame strictly religious people for violence, but the skeptic in me sees selfishness and brutality as a pan-human problem. The skeptic in me suspects Jesus was right on this: no one is good but God.

The skeptic in me hears people say, "All paths lead to God," but finds this wanting. It sure seems like most of them just lead right back to me.

And if there are plenty of other paths to God, there's no reason for the cross to have been such a bloody affair at all.

> If there are plenty of other paths to God, there's no reason for the cross to have been such a bloody affair at all.

So where else do I go?

Yes, I certainly see the things done with the label "Christian" that have absolutely nothing to do with Christ, like the hurts from my own pastor-led family, but does irreligion have the answer? As the West gets more "post-Christian," are we getting happier?

We're more affluent than ever, sure. But happier? Jonathan Haidt, in his book *The Happiness Hypothesis*, says there's no reason to believe we are.

As the level of wealth has doubled or tripled in the last fifty years in many industrialized nations, the levels of happiness and satisfaction with life that people report have not changed, and depression has actually become more common.[6]

I just read something remarkable about our drug problem. It's historic: more Americans are now dying from heroin than from gun homicides. Robert Anderson with the Centers for Disease Control and Prevention said, "I don't think we've ever seen anything like this. Certainly not in modern times."[7]

More heroin deaths than gun homicides. That's remarkable.

Suicides, on the other hand, have skyrocketed.

Ross Douthat, a columnist for the *New York Times*, wrote that the United States is getting less violent in "every way save one":

> As Americans commit fewer and fewer crimes against other people's lives and property, they have become more likely to inflict fatal violence on themselves.
>
> In the 1990s, the suicide rate dipped with the crime rate. But since 2000, it has risen, and jumped particularly sharply among the middle-aged. The suicide rate for Americans 35 to 54 increased nearly 30 percent between 1999 and 2010; for men in their 50s, it rose nearly 50 percent. More Americans now die of suicide than in car accidents, and gun suicides are almost twice as common as gun homicides.[8]

No, we're not getting happier.

We're getting lonelier.

Again, this chapter isn't meant as an irrefutable argument for God. (One can't make an irrefutable argument for anything, really.) It's just that so many of us are one-way skeptics.

We find that religion "doesn't work" without seeing the obvious: irreligion doesn't work either.

For some of us, even those of us lacking emotional reward from our belief in God, it's like we've taken the red pill. We've seen the Matrix. The world doesn't add up.

Gerald May wrote about how this happens among cultural misfits:

> Not uncommonly this dawning awareness happens intermittently over the course of a lifetime, as I have described it. But it can happen at any time. Some people even seem to have been born with it. They grow up trying to adjust themselves to the values and strivings that surround them, but somehow their hearts are never in it. They have a deep awareness that fulfillment cannot be found through acquisition and achievement. They often feel like misfits because of the different, deeper, ungraspable love they feel inside them. For them, the journey is not so much toward realization of their desire as toward being able to claim the desire they already have in a culture that neither understands nor supports it.[9]

Yes, I could walk away from Jesus, but I'm not sure who else has the words of life.

Honestly, it seems like the world is achingly lonely for Him. Like we can all sense it. We know something isn't right.

You should know something about this particular God, the God of the Bible, and it's immediately apparent in the first words of Genesis, even if we don't notice it.

Now, in other ancient creation stories, the universe is the result of revenge, or incest, or wars, or murderous plots. The sun, the mountains, the trees . . . everything is the result of some violent clash. For example, in the Enuma Elish, which is a Babylonian account of creation believed to have been written in the twelfth to eighteenth centuries BC, the world is made out of a lot of conflict, to put it mildly.

Briefly: There's the freshwater god, Apsu, and the saltwater god, Tiamat. There are additional gods, and they live inside Tiamat. They make a lot of noise, which ticks off both Tiamat and Apsu. So Apsu wants to kill them.

But the most powerful god, named Ea, kills Apsu. Ea then has a son named Marduk, who's the new greatest god. He likes to make tornadoes. This causes problems for Tiamat, who still can't get any sleep because the gods living inside her are bothered by all the loud stuff Marduk is doing.

So Tiamat makes eleven monsters to help her get revenge for Apsu's death. Other gods aren't happy about this, so they make Marduk their champion. He kills Tiamat.

And then he forms the world out of her corpse.

(And this explains why you haven't seen *The Marduk and Tiamat Puppet Show*.)

Anyway, in Genesis, God makes the world because He *wants* to, and He *loves* each part of it. He makes this, and it's "good." He makes that, and it's "good." The way it's written is clearly in overt contrast with the Enuma Elish. This God is different, and He loves what He made. All of it.

The world was full of gods, but this one identifies Himself this stunning way, in Exodus 15:26: *"I am the* LORD, *who heals you."*

This God is the healing God.

As repulsed as I might be by Christian hypocrisy, including my own, I am very attracted to a God who heals. Healing isn't a side issue. When Jesus walked among us, it's how He demonstrated His very identity: A lame man walks. A girl is raised from the dead.

> **As repulsed as I might be by Christian hypocrisy, including my own, I am very attracted to a God who heals.**

When John the Baptist's own faith wavered, Jesus sent people to remind Him of the healings. The blind see. The deaf hear. That means the kingdom of the healing God is here.

I could look elsewhere, but to whom else would I go? Jesus, after all, is the God who heals little girls.

No, I do not want to walk away from this. On the contrary, I want to be part of it, doubts and questions and all.

Thankfully, Scripture also reveals a God who is patient with people like me. In the book of Jude, we're even told to be merciful to people who doubt.

So I memorized that verse. "Be merciful to those who doubt" (Jude v. 22).

I like to memorize really short verses.

Today I got a text about a friend/acquaintance in a high-profile, big-stage church ministry. He was just busted for having an affair. It made me nauseous, especially for both families involved.

I decided to make a quick, informal count of people I've personally known, in similar ministries, who've gone through that, and came up with fifteen. I'm sure I'll think of more.

Rich Mullins once said, "No, the church isn't full of hypocrites. We always have room for more."

It's tough to take. I know we're all moral failures, but . . . yikes.

But also today I got an e-mail at work, this one about "The Girl with the Red Feet."

Her real name is Habeeba. She's six.

She was born with clubfeet, which means her feet are turned inward, like golf clubs. As a result, she's never been able to walk normally. Her parents are poor, but desperately wanted her to be healed. It hurt them deeply to see the heartbreak their daughter endured, being mocked by other kids and even adults. They were also told her disability would disqualify her from going to school.

The girl's mom didn't want her daughter to be so ashamed. So she had an idea: she would decorate her daughter's feet to make them beautiful. She wanted her to smile when she looked at them.

She dyed her feet in red henna, and she drew little cartoons on her feet. Anything to make Habeeba less ashamed.

Again, more heartbreak. Her mom now saw her daughter

was also mocked for her red feet. She was even made fun of by her own cousins as "The Girl with the Red Feet." More shame.

They found out about a surgery that would heal her, but it was costly, and with just one income—her dad is a bus driver—they had no money. So they had a two-year plan: They would all skip at least one meal a day, and they would leave their own small, rented apartment and cram in with another family in their tiny apartment. It would take two years of saving, but they could eventually afford the surgery.

The time came. They gave everything they had.

The surgery was a failure.

Everything was lost.

Thankfully, the story doesn't end there. The mom and dad found out about CURE's clubfoot program, and now Habeeba is being properly treated.

And the cost? Nothing.

She's in a series of casts now, as her legs are being made straight.

They're all thrilled. They didn't understand how it couldn't cost anything. How could this be free? The answer they got from the CURE staff is simple: God loves Habeeba, so God's people do too. They gave of themselves to make it happen.

———

Where else do I go?

I can't escape the sense that there is transcendent purpose in life.

I can't escape the sense that Habeeba objectively *matters*, even if the world never knew about her.

I can't escape the sense that our very longing for things—true justice, peace, rest—is because we're made for it. We're really designed that way. We're nostalgic for a place we've never been. We see little breakthroughs, little hints of the kingdom, and we get goose bumps. "For they are not the thing itself; they are only the scent of a flower we have not found, the echo of a tune we have not heard, news from a country we have never yet visited," wrote C. S. Lewis.[10]

I can't walk away. I still have questions, but I still believe:

Death really is *not* the last word.

Love and the decision to sacrifice your own interests for others really are *not* reducible to mere chemical reactions.

Many things that seem "evil" really *are* evil.

That evil really *will* be defeated.

There *will*, in the end, be justice.

There *is* a Lover of your very soul.

And like so many great stories that span cultures and time, there *is* a good King, after all, who still wants us.

Something I've noticed over the years: those who think these things are false, those who think I'm wrong?

Deep down, *they're hoping I'm right.*

NINETEEN

Blessed Are the Unnoticed

ONCE, ON A SUNDAY MORNING IN A NEW TOWN, MY wife and I tried to make some friends.

We went online to find a new church and showed up in time for a Sunday school class. We walked in a room with four or five other couples sitting in a circle.

No one acknowledged us. I didn't mind so much, because it meant I didn't have to try small talk, but it was a little odd. It was a small room. I started noticing they weren't even looking at us.

The leader began teaching, and he didn't look at us either. It was apparent they all knew one another. My wife and I felt like we were intruders, but it started actually getting amusing. Now it was just a matter of, "How long will they go before acknowledging our existence?"

I can now answer that question: it took six years.

It was painful, but we had to laugh. We went to the massive worship service, and no one talked to us there either, except the greeter, and that's nice, but I've been around church long enough to know the greeter is assigned to greet everybody. He has no choice. He's the greeter. Greeters gonna greet.

And yes, six years later, we went back.

In the interim, I became Christian-famous in the area as a quirky radio host. I was kind of a big deal apparently. I was invited to come to the church, and we were seated in the front row, and the pastor pointed me out before the sermon.

He had us stand, and everybody clapped for me because I'm Brant Hansen and, clearly, I should be clapped for. It felt pretty good.

Afterward, I told them, as kindly as I could, that it was all a bit odd, because when I was there before, no one talked to me, and now I was being celebrated. But the thing is, I told them, *I'm actually still the same guy.*

I guess celebrities get celebrated, and I sure like being celebrated.

It made me think about a couple things. For one, I bet everybody would like to be celebrated.

The other thing I thought about was how someday I won't be on the radio anymore.

I wonder if people will still talk to me.

———————

Jesus takes the idea that we should treat some as more important than others and He burns it down, salts the fields around it, dissolves the whole thing in acid, and then hits it with a hydrogen bomb . . . and then we decide to do it anyway.

For example: He says we shouldn't use religious titles

(Matt. 23:8–12). I'm but a simple man, so I don't understand all the theological and cultural complexities. But apparently higher minds than mine have unpacked the nuance behind, "Don't use religious titles," and found that He meant, roughly, "Hey, you guys should totally use religious titles!"

We love this stuff. We love elevating ourselves, we love being significant, and we love making idols of people. The desire to believe that this athlete, or that singer, or this popular church speaker has somehow made it spiritually is a force of human nature.

Yes, God is at work, but if the Bible is any indication of how He actually operates, He's at work on the margins, not on the stages.

We're watching the lights, cameras, and action . . . and He's at work precisely where we're not looking.

> Yes, God is at work, but if the Bible is any indication of how He actually operates, He's at work on the margins, not on the stages.

I once met this guy named Kumar when I visited DC. He was thirty-six, had a wife and kids, and worked in an office as a computer engineer at a big tech company.

My friend Woody introduced me to him and we walked to Whole Foods, got some salads, and then sat and talked.

Kumar goes to a church that meets in a school gym just outside DC. He and his wife sit in the partly filled rows of folding chairs. The pastor there has a Big Vision for reaching the area, including a plan to buy forty acres in suburban DC, which could be really pricey. Maybe a few hundred million?

Anyway, Kumar told me he was once on a bus in Chennai, India, and it was crammed with people. But he heard God's voice. "Unmistakably, I heard this. I heard God say, twice, 'Seek Me.' That was it. Twice."

"Just 'Seek Me'?"

"Yes, just 'Seek Me.' And I knew it was God, but which God? I was Hindu," he said. "It could have been Vishnu or Kali, or . . . ? I didn't know. I just knew it was God. Somehow I knew it. Unmistakable."

Of course, I'm skeptical about this sort of thing. It's worth pointing out that Kumar says he's skeptical by nature too. He has advanced degrees in aerospace engineering and physics from a top university.

He was baffled by what happened. He made it a point of study and wasn't satisfied that it could be attributed to one of his familiar gods. He found a friend with a Bible, who considered it a good-luck charm, and he traded a textbook for it.

Kumar started reading the Bible ("I found it quite confusing," he said. I told him I still do too sometimes) and eventually became a Jesus-follower.

That was a very costly decision.

His parents were greatly displeased. They scheduled an arranged marriage. Kumar met his wife-to-be on Friday, told her and his parents on Saturday about his Jesus decision, and got married on Sunday.

"They thought it would blow over," he said.

It didn't.

Six months later, there was an intervention. Apparently it was the Family Reunion from Heck. And it wasn't just family; it was friends and neighbors too. They surrounded him, telling him to repudiate his faith. He didn't.

"My parents said I need to leave right now. They were scared for their reputation," Kumar told me. "They would simply tell everyone I was dead."

He took a job in the United States. He drove to a big church building.

"I didn't know what else to do," he said. "Nice cars everywhere. I liked that."

He walked in and was shocked. "It was a fancy church, and everyone was a black person, and they were quite animated. They were walking on their chairs around the room. I was confused, but they were happy.

"They had a testimony time, and I like microphones, so I got up and told them, 'I am so happy about Jesus! I do not want a Mercedes or a BMW! I want to go back to India to tell people about Jesus!' Everyone applauded me! I was the center of attention! But I had just lied! I did not want to go back.

"Actually, I did want to be rich. I did want a Mercedes."

But some guys took him to a room and prayed with him. They asked God to help him make his return back to India.

"But I did not want to go back to India . . ."

A few years later, he went back to India.

"I took a vacation from work and headed over to tell people about Jesus."

"Just tell people about Jesus? What was the plan?"

"I didn't have a plan. I just landed and went to a neighborhood and I went door-to-door and I started telling people."

The first day, forty-five people decided to become Jesus-followers.

"How'd *that* happen?"

"I don't know. I just went door-to-door, and neighbors would introduce me to others, and I was amazed."

Kumar said he still heads to India on his vacations. But things have grown. From those first forty-five, and from his trips over the past seven years . . .

More than one hundred thousand conversions. One hundred thirty-nine new Christian communities. Model orphanages for children suffering from AIDS. Schools for Dalit children, the lowest-of-the-low in India. Shelters for little girls, now rescued from prostitution. Food. Medicine. More telling people about the Jesus Who Talks to People Like Kumar on Crowded Buses.

They want to name projects after Kumar. He does not allow them. He and his wife spend hours every day, after work, praying and communicating and wondering what the next move is.

He doesn't actively raise financial support. Not his style, apparently.

"God always provides. Children are hungry in a project, because all we have is rice for them, and not much. But Woody gave us some money for a down payment on four acres with hundreds of coconut trees, and then several families who know us each called me, unaware of what we were doing. 'God woke us up last night, and we can't get you off our mind. Here's five thousand dollars . . . Here's a thousand dollars . . .' We got the forty-thousand we needed to buy the land. I am always amazed."

I told him I didn't get it. "So . . . we made a quantum leap in your story. Forty-five people decide to follow Jesus, and now more than one hundred thousand. Wha . . . ? How . . . ?"

We sat at our table in our hotel room, and Kumar started laughing. I laughed too—and then I realized he wasn't laughing. He was crying, and he couldn't speak.

"So many have died . . ."

"Who has died?"

"So many of our pastors, so many of our people . . ."

I looked at Woody, who knows the stories, and he bit his lip and nodded.

Kumar: "They are beaten to death, they are killed, because they are talking about Jesus. It happens all the time in India, but the country is very concerned about image, very concerned about foreign investment, so they pretend it doesn't happen.

"They are the reason this growth has happened. Their blood. I ask God, 'Why do You let this happen to these people who love You?' They have nothing. Our pastors are not paid. There is no money. But I realized, God is releasing them at last. They have nothing, they are beaten, they are hungry, they live on the ground, in the streets, and God finally releases them to go home."

He paused for a long time. And I didn't know what to say either.

Woody, who met Kumar at that church with big plans in

suburban DC, said I should let Kumar eat his salad. He was right. It was getting late. It was a long meal.

If you're reading this on a weekday, Kumar is sitting in a little room doing his tech job, and he's also answering e-mails from India when he gets a break. And he prays. On Sundays, he sits on a folding chair in a high school gym, and he hears about the church's big plans. It will be costly, but a new building could make a big difference.

He admitted he wonders sometimes, "They have now added us to the missions budget. They give $1,000 per year. I guess I'm happy for that, but . . ." And he didn't finish the sentence.

I can finish it. But I don't want to.

> **I've always thought if something *true* violates my theology, well, I should change my theology.**

I think about Kumar a lot. I think about how refreshing it is that God uses the unexpected people, the humble people, and how He promises to bring the big shots down low.

God has favorites, you know. Most church people deny it, because it violates their theology, but I've always thought if something *true* violates my theology, well, I should change my theology.

He favors the humble. He opposes the proud. This is said

overtly and repeatedly in the Bible, and it's demonstrated in a hundred stories. This is clearly how He operates.

> Listen to me, dear brothers and sisters. Hasn't God chosen the poor in this world to be rich in faith? Aren't they the ones who will inherit the Kingdom he promised to those who love him? (James 2:5 NLT)

> God chose things despised by the world, things counted as nothing at all, and used them to bring to nothing what the world considers important. (1 Cor. 1:28 NLT)

God's preference for the humble is a big turnoff for people who aren't humble.

This takes us back to atheist Richard Dawkins, who certainly has a problem with it.

> Of course I have doubts all the time, and I think in a way the word "atheism" is misleading because it suggests that there's just one alternative, which is God. I'm constantly on the alert for changes of mind, but extremely skeptical that those changes will just happen to be in the direction of embracing a god of Bronze Age camel herders from the Middle East.[1]

Surely a self-respecting God wouldn't choose camel herders. Maybe herders of some other kind of animal, sure, but certainly not from the Bronze Age, of all ages. And not from the Middle East. Let's be realistic. C'mon.

Clearly, any legitimate god would opt for more qualified

people, like, say, wealthy, modern, enlightened British biology professors.

But the God of the Bible says He didn't choose these Bronze Age camel herders because they were impressive. He chose them, in part, because they *weren't*.

> For you are a holy people to the LORD your God; the LORD your God has chosen you to be a people for Himself, a special treasure above all the peoples on the face of the earth. The LORD did not set His love on you nor choose you because you were more in number than any other people, for you were the least of all peoples; but because the LORD loves you, and because He would keep the oath which He swore to your fathers, the LORD has brought you out with a mighty hand, and redeemed you from the house of bondage, from the hand of Pharaoh king of Egypt. (Deut. 7:6–8 NKJV)

God didn't choose to share the good news of Jesus' birth first with shepherds because they were key societal influencers.

God didn't choose Nazareth as Jesus' hometown because it was a cultural hub, bustling with seminary-trained, catalytic thought-leaders.

Jesus had plenty of options for disciples. There was no shortage of religious experts, well-known communicators, and known leaders in His area . . . but He recruited some fishermen. This was not an accident.

The first Christian missionary in history was not a powerful speaker with funny stories who had the ability to organize big outreaches at the local stadium. It was a woman (!) with a terrible sexual reputation. A woman who not only couldn't attract crowds, she had to avoid them out of shame.

She had no credentials. She believed the wrong things. She was from the wrong place and part of the wrong race.

Yet Jesus chose her (John 4).

You're a misfit? Good. That's exactly the sort of person God uses. And when it happens, you probably won't get credit from The Important People. No one besides God Himself may notice. But the seemingly miscast are the people He chooses.

> You're a misfit? Good. That's exactly the sort of person God uses.

But what about David? He was an awesome leader! A great warrior king! God chose him, right?

Yes, God chose him. But David was the runt of the litter. Even though God had warned His people earlier that they were better off without a king, yes, God chose David, the unimpressive shepherd boy, whose brothers were impressive leader material. They were the ones who seemed destined for greatness. No one saw the anointing of David coming. Everyone was shocked.

That was the point.

But what about Moses? He was strong and handsome and—

No, that was Charlton Heston. Moses was eighty years old when God picked him.

So powerful is our desire to elevate the good-looking and strong that we can't even countenance movies that feature eighty-year-old heroes. Instead, we must cast Heston or Christian Bale.

God, however, is apparently okay with casting eighty-year-olds. He favors the humble and opposes the proud. It's not because younger people weren't around. It's because God does things His way.

I saw a website advertising a major annual Christian conference. It attracts thousands of—apparently—very, very impressive people, because it says it's for "the doers," the "cultural architects," the "influencers," the "change agents," the "bold," the "excellent," those who are "passionate about something big," and the "driven."

I guess I'm out. I can't even organize my sock drawer.

I'd also honestly be *afraid* of considering myself a driven, bold cultural architect, because I'd wonder if I was disqualifying myself from the actual work. Bold cultural architects may do some neat things, but they don't seem the type God chooses.

It seems like being "passionate for something big" is something positive, but I keep running into Jesus telling us to be like children.

And children are small. Maybe you've noticed that too. They do little things, and they're okay with it. They like it, even.

Jesus seems passionate about other little things too. Mustard seeds. Sparrows. Lilies of the field.

Single days, like today, instead of The Big Future. Little acts of our will.

Things like that.

I have a theory about those Big Leader conferences. Actually, it's more of a vision: God is searching, always searching, and He's looking to use people for something wonderful, and He scans the packed conference arena, looking up and down the aisles of self-styled driven change agents.

He sees the bold . . . and the educated . . . and the change-agent, leading thinkers. All qualified. Charismatic. Dynamic. One after the other.

And He picks no one.

That is, until the lights are dimmed, the place is empty, and there's a fifty-year-old Hispanic lady, and she's picking up their garbage, and He smiles and says . . .

"Ah, that's the one."

TWENTY

Blessed Are the Lonely

I ONCE INTERVIEWED A MAN ON MY RADIO SHOW who'd been a counselor for decades and who was now a professor of psychology.

He said there were a lot of reasons why people seek counseling, but at least 90 percent of the people he'd seen, deep down, were there for the same reason: they're lonely.

Seriously? Ninety percent?

I never forgot that. So each time I talked with someone in the counseling field, I asked them if they thought it was true, that we really are that lonely. I've never had one disagree with the first man's estimate.

That is, except for a counselor I met recently. He has a unique practice: he counsels celebrities, including the household-name variety. They're people admired by millions and celebrated at every turn. So I asked him what he thought of the 90 percent figure.

"No, not for me. It's more like 100 percent."

Really?

"Really, that's why people want to talk to me. They're being crushed by loneliness. It's rampant, and being a celebrity just makes it worse."

I thought of something Anne Hathaway said in a very honest interview. She's a beautiful actress and an amazing talent. So what's her biggest fear?

> Loneliness is my least favorite thing about life. The thing that I'm most worried about is just being alone without anybody to care for or someone who will care for me.[1]

I think she's being honest. And I think if we, too, are being honest, we'd say we understand. The drive to avoid loneliness animates much of our behavior, I suspect.

Loneliness is powerful, but rarely acknowledged. I suspect loneliness, at least in part, explains why you're reading these words even now.

And I suspect loneliness, at least in part, is why I'm writing them.

The *New York Times* says we're living during an "epidemic of loneliness,"[2] and we can all come up with our own theories about why our culture has come to this. But I want to make it clear that if you're lonely, you're hardly alone.

I'm not going to fix our loneliness in this short chapter. But we can look at how God feels about it.

In the Bible, there's a story about a girl from Egypt. We don't know much about her, except that she left her homeland and became a slave for a woman named Sarah. The girl's name was Hagar. It's a bizarre story (you can read it in Genesis 16), and it's heartbreaking. Sarah and her husband, Abraham, have no children. Sarah believes she's too old to have a child, so she hands over Hagar to Abraham to bear his child.

Abraham sleeps with Hagar, but he clearly doesn't care about her. Sarah now finds Hagar's presence antagonizing. Neither seems to want her around.

So Hagar runs away. She finds herself alone, and pregnant, in the desert.

But then there's a surprise appearance: The "Angel of the Lord" shows up for the very first time in the Bible. The Angel of the Lord tells this girl, this lonely, powerless slave, that the Lord has heard her cries. She's not alone after all.

Hagar, given her background, surely knew the stories of many gods. But she comes up with her own name for this one, this God who actually cared about her enough to seek her out and speak to her.

This misfit calls Him, "The God Who Sees Me."

Oddly, I just read about another Egyptian girl, another misfit. She's probably about the same age too.

This story isn't three thousand years old. It just happened. I know about it because I get daily e-mails at work from CURE International's hospitals and programs, updating me on patients who come through the doors.

So I just read this report about Amira. She's used a wheelchair her whole life. She was born with a disability. She's been told that God cursed her, but she never believed it, because her dad told her otherwise.

He was relentlessly positive. He always told her she would get better, and she'd be able to run and play someday, just like her friends. He would see to it, he said. Someday they'd be able to find a doctor, someone they could afford, and she would be healed.

Her dad was a dreamer. He was her light and her inspiration.

Until she was twelve, when her father died in a car accident.

Her mom remarried, and the man she married was appalled at the idea of having a girl with a disability in his home. He didn't want to be cursed as well. So he made Amira's mom choose: Would it be him, or Amira? She made a devastating decision.

Amira was dropped off at an orphanage.

The orphanage was for kids with disabilities. Some were blind, some mentally disabled; others, like her, were unable to walk.

The woman who took care of the kids, a Christian woman named Larnia, saw Amira's broken heart. Larnia told Amira about a verse in the Bible that I'd never even noticed before I read this story. Now I'll never forget it:

> Can a mother forget the baby at her breast
>> and have no compassion on the child she has borne?
> Though she may forget,
>> I will not forget you! (Isa. 49:15)

She reminded Amira, the abandoned girl, of the verse over and over, of God's promise: *Though your mother may forget you . . . I won't.*

Larnia heard about CURE and took Amira to them so that, at fifteen years old, she could get a life-changing surgery to straighten her legs.

After the surgery, everyone in the orphanage gathered in Amira's room. Kids who couldn't see. Kids who couldn't talk.

And lo, there was a great party.

Amira told the CURE staff that she thinks her Father in heaven made her dad's dreams come true.

This is how God feels about the lonely. He sees you. He has not forgotten you.

"Though your mother may forget you . . . I won't."

There are many promises in the Bible, but one gets repeated more than any other. It makes me again suspect God know us very well, indeed:

"I will be with you."

He knew about people like us. He knew that even those of us who accepted His proposal, who drank from His cup, would wonder where He went.

So He says it over

He knew about people like us. He knew that even those of us who accepted His proposal, who drank from His cup, would wonder where He went.

and over, so many times that even people like me can get it: *I will be with you.*

I think Jesus knew we'd be lonely and we would need to be reminded. But given our understanding of the betrothal period we're in, at least we can know *why* we're lonely and *why* we're yearning.

I get the impression that most of the world is lonely without knowing why. But ours can be a longing that's accompanied by something that simply can't be underestimated in its power: hope.

We can acknowledge the loneliness, understand it, feel it deeply . . . and yet look forward with anticipation.

I know how I'm supposed to conclude this discussion. I'm supposed to write something like, "So if you truly believe in God, you won't ever be lonely anymore," or something like that.

Even if this were a children's book, I wouldn't do that, because it's not true. In fact, the stronger my faith becomes, the more I might ache to be closer with God. I can find contentment in the sense that I no longer thirst for more significance, attention, respect, or a nicer house. But there's a discontent that comes with knowing God. The more I get a sense of what His kingdom is like, the more I want to see it in full.

Loneliness can coexist with faith. It's not that God isn't the very best Lover of our souls; I believe He is. It's just that we humans are all designed for a home we haven't been to yet.

He tells us to trust Him a thousand ways, knowing our dark, lonely nights of the soul may be long indeed.

Here's a text a listener sent to my radio show:

I'm trying to hear God's voice. I'm trying to listen. I've read that God is always speaking. I want something that isn't a whimper. Something personal. Something I cannot deny or doubt.

Everything I believe says God wants the same thing. So what is the problem?[3]

This was the best response I could muster on the air. (And no, I couldn't text this back. Not sure my data plan would've covered it.)

I wish I knew your name.

And I wish I knew your name because . . . my response would sound so much better. Bad news usually does. "I'm afraid you're asking for something you can't yet have" seems somehow harsher than, say, "Tara, I'm afraid you're asking for something you can't yet have."

But it's true. You can't have it. Not yet.

Here, and now, I'm convinced there's not a thing God could communicate to you that you can't deny. Nothing He could say would be incontrovertible. And no matter what He did, what miracle He showed you . . . ? You could rebel against it. This is the reality of where we are, now.

Check out the stories in the Bible. People got pillars of fire, and it took about a half-hour before they were bowing down to a golden calf. More "denial"? Peter, one of Jesus' best friends, got to see miracle after miracle, and his name is now synonymous with the word, "deny," itself. Doubt?

John the Baptist, himself, doubted who Jesus was, after personally baptizing Him.

God fixed the stars in the sky, and holds every atom together. He's so masterful, our doubt itself is a miracle: Our very consciousness remains unexplained. But doubt, and deny, we do.

You want something that makes it impossible for you to doubt. Problem is, you're human, and humans can doubt anything. The clear voice of God, itself, can be doubted. ("Was that really Him, really?" "Couldn't that have been a neural misfire?" "You know, maybe that 'miracle' years ago was a coincidence . . .")

You want something you can't have . . . yet.

But now . . . the good news:

It seems like you really want more of God. And, from what I read, that's a really good thing. You're going to get what you're looking for.

If you're frustrated now, you're in great company. Just look at the Psalms, for instance. David, who wrote many of them, was a man "after God's own heart" and yet he was left wondering, often, "God, where did you go? Why did you hide your face?" He was left with yearning.

Or look at Paul, whom Jesus recruited with all the subtlety of a two-by-four to the head. Paul had the miracle, the light from Heaven, the conversation with Jesus . . . and still said we can only see dimly, now, what we will one day see in full. He was left with yearning.

If you want more of God, you're going to yearn. And yearning isn't bad. Yearning happens when you love. Lovers yearn, when they want, but they cannot fully have. Not yet.

Lovers yearn, but religious people don't.

Religious people want their rules, and they have them in full. There's nothing to yearn for. (In fact, when they're honest, the only thing they might yearn for is a way out.)

But God calls us to relationship, and that means yearning.

Want to experience yearning in another context? Try being engaged to be married, but living a chaste life. I've done it. It's hard. You yearn, and you know what you want, and you know you're going to get what you want . . . but not yet. You want more . . . but not yet.

It's really, really tough. And, tough as it is, it's really, really good. Yearning like that—that powerful—only happens because the object of the yearning is that powerful.

And let's face it. I said "yearning in another context," but you know what? It's really not another context: We are promised, in the end, a wedding. Jesus will have His bride, and it's His people. And He will know us, and we will know Him, fully. Paul wrote as much: "Then I shall know just as I also am known."

So you're yearning, and so are we all, but it's building up to something. Something really, really good.

You're engaged, and the wedding is going to be one amazing party, and knowing God, finally, and truly, is going to be worth it.

There's nothing wrong with yearning for it.[4]

In the meantime, we may be lonely, but He promises we are not alone.

He is the God who sees us.

And though others may forget us . . . He won't.

Blessed Are the Misfit Royalty

OCCASIONALLY, BECAUSE OF MY JOB, I'M ASKED TO take part in a Christian Award Show of some sort or another. I politely decline.

It's not that they're evil or anything. Probably.

I mean, there are some really nice people involved. And red carpets, and photographers, and everybody gets cleaned up and looks super-nice.

I just genuinely don't understand them. They don't compute. It's the same people every year, and it's spotlights and stages and "Best Artist" categories, and these are people who make their living getting attention. I think that's kind of dangerous for them.

I once saw a show on TV called *Gifted*. I wondered what it was all about, and I thought I might relate since I was placed in the Gifted class in our little football-crazed high school. (In that context, *gifted* meant, quite clearly, "Please pummel me.")

On this show, though, *gifted* meant that they were super-duper Christians who loved to sing onstage. It was modeled after *American Idol*, but these singers were a "better" crop of people. I know this because of the bios for each of the finalists. One young lady had a "love for Christ that is unparalleled," and that's pretty impressive, if you think about it.

Anyway, I don't really understand a lot of Christian things. Someone once said that the word *Christian* makes for a lousy adjective, and I thought, *That's so true.*

Until I received an invitation to a very particular Christian red-carpet event.

I rented a tux for it and combed my hair and everything. People know me from the radio, and I'm an author and whatnot, so I tried to look good. People were to arrive in limousines, and the red carpet would be lined with paparazzi.

It was all very swank. Catered meal and everything.

I was a little anxious on the way over. My wife and I got out of the car, and I nervously straightened my tie. It was going to be a big night.

As we reached the door, I was given a box. Inside was shoeshine, a cloth, and a brush. My job for the night? Shoeshine guy. It's my favorite part of what's called "Night to Shine."

Minutes later, they started filing in. First a few, then dozens, then a huge crowd, all people with special needs. This was their night. And as they arrived, I would shine shoes, other volunteers would check hair and help with makeup, and then our guests would be announced, one by one, before walking down the red carpet.

The "paparazzi" were also volunteers. The limousines were rented for all the special guests—the "kings" and "queens," as the organizers called them. The first-class catered meal wasn't for us; it was for the royalty.

After shining shoes, I got to stand along the red carpet and hoot and holler for each announced guest. Teenagers, young adults, even senior citizens; some walking with braces, some with walkers, others in wheelchairs, who'd never been celebrated before. They'd never been treated like royalty.

I remember one young lady in a beautiful blue, Cinderella-type dress being announced. People turned to look at her, and there was an audible gasp at how she looked in her tiara and dress. She looked stunned by the attention and stood there to soak it all in. As she slowly walked forward, I heard people saying—and I'm sure she heard it too—"Oh my, she's so beautiful."

And after they finished the great banquet, the DJ started the dance. It's part of "Night to Shine" events at churches all across the country. All upbeat music. No slow songs. Just the way I like it.

I got to dance the way I like: as a goofball. I got the impression no one was judging me. No one was trying to be cool. I even tried my regionally famous "Russian Kick Dance" to some Jackson 5. I feel like that ministered to people in a special way.

Best party I've ever been to. I'm not exaggerating. Hands-down. My wife thought so too.

I remember talking to her on the way home. So much of church stuff I just don't get.

"Now this—this I understand."

———

Once there was a woman, an expectant mom, riding a very crowded bus. The bus slipped off a roadway in a rainstorm into a ravine. Everyone on board died, except her.

There was an emergency surgery. The baby, a little boy, was saved.

As he grew, it was apparent that he was very strong willed. As a result, his father kicked him out of the house at fourteen years old. He left home and became a brilliant man and a natural leader.

Normally, at this point in a story like this, I'd tell you the man's name, and you'd recognize it, because he's famous. Maybe he became a king, or perhaps he's now a US senator or an astronaut or a famous athlete. He is none of those things.

His name is Emmanuel, and he is Nigerian. When his father kicked him out for becoming a Christian, he still managed to get an education. All his kids now have college educations too.

What Emmanuel does with his life, by choice, is something almost no one else will do.

He brings dignity to the shamed.

Emmanuel works at the CURE hospital in Mbale, Uganda. He works with children who have spina bifida, kids who can't relieve their own bowels. They, and their families, often stay hidden. They are desperately vulnerable.

Emmanuel uses a medical procedure to bring relief to the child by cleaning their bowels, and he does it in a way that leaves the family feeling somehow dignified. It's something so few are ever willing to do, and it's pure mercy. My friend Derek worked with Emmanuel for a decade and was "always amazed."

"These are often kids who aren't babies. They're eight years old. They live their whole lives in shame. The parents are ashamed, because having a child with any disability is seen as a curse. These kids experience shame on shame," Derek said.

"And here's this remarkable, strong man who puts the whole family at ease. He gets down on their level. They've never had anyone treat their child with dignity, with respect. This is a low spot in their lives, and he knows it. It's a difficult, dirty job, and he's done it for fifteen years, every day. His love for people is profound. I've never seen anything quite like it."

> **We keep elevating the seemingly flawless, the beautiful, the "clean." Emmanuel elevates the disabled, the shamed, the dirty.**

We keep elevating the seemingly flawless, the beautiful, the "clean." Emmanuel elevates the disabled, the shamed, the dirty.

Every kingdom has royalty.

We bow before ours, and Emmanuel bows before his.

Sometimes I think about how God identifies with the weak and the vulnerable, and it makes me really thankful. Oddly enough, it makes me think about how we humans like to identify with sports teams.

I noticed this early on and wanted to be part of the whole sports scene. So I chose to play a fun game called baseball.

Some background: baseball is when they let you pick out

a metal bat and then make you stay in a little box while the biggest kid in town, Brad Francisco, throws a rock-hard ball 400 mph and hits you in the head.

I didn't get a hit my first year. It was hard for me to see the ball because of my eye problems. But did I give up? No, I did not give up. I kept the dream alive.

I did not get a hit my second season either. Or the third. But I did not want to be a quitter.

I also did not get a hit during my fourth year of organized baseball. (I did put a ball in play that year. It was a pop fly that was caught. The crowd audibly gasped when I made contact. I remember that. And I remember the hard-throwing pitcher, whose name was Tricia.)

I continued to play. My fifth season concluded with zero hits. My sixth and seventh seasons didn't go very well either.

In all, my statistics are as follows: eight years, zero hits. That's right: I was oh-for-eight years. (If you are into statistics and you run the numbers, you'll see that my batting average works out to .000 with a slugging percentage of .000.)

This isn't a sad story at all, because I was actually given a trophy as the league's "Mr. Hustle" one year. To this day, I'm baffled how I managed to "hustle" without leaving the confines of the batter's box, but I have a trophy and they can't have it back.

Anyway, my point is that people love sports and take them really seriously.

In fact, I remember a study that said winning teams help our self-esteem, particularly for guys. Another study looked at single men and found that after their favorite football team wins, they're likely to rate *themselves* as more attractive.[1]

So it's pretty simple, really. The logic is as follows:

1. I'm a fan of Team X.
2. Team X won a game.
3. Conclusion: I'm suddenly good-looking.

We humans get our identities so caught up with our sports teams that when they win, we think more highly of ourselves.

We bias reality too. I once saw a football play where two players came down with a pass. One guy was on the Packers, the other on the Seahawks. All the Packers fans thought the Packers guy caught the ball. All the Seahawks fans thought the Seahawks guy caught the ball.

I mean, they genuinely believed that. Both sets of fans could pass lie detector tests. Same play, totally different perceptions, split evenly down team lines. When humans identify with someone, we're biased. We apparently can't help it.

What's more, we try to physically look like our team. We wear colors and logos we normally would never wear. People don't wear shirts with drawings of giant, orange, disembodied bear heads unless there's an identity thing going on.

Where our identity goes, our money follows. We not only buy the hat, we buy the tickets or the cable TV package, pay for the trip to the stadium, all that. Our resources go where our hearts are.

We pick our favorites, and we identify with them. We have our team.

So does God, apparently. He loves us all, but identifies with particular people. Misfits. That's His team.

"He raises the poor from the dust," the Bible says in

1 Samuel 2:8. And Psalm 9:18 promises, "God will never forget the needy."

Psalm 72:4 declares that He will "defend the afflicted." And God will "defend the weak," says Psalm 82:3.

In Matthew 25 Jesus described the hungry, the thirsty, the prisoners, and the sick, and then said if you've done something for them, "the least of these brothers and sisters of mine," you've done it to Him. He's directly identifying with particular people.

There's a proverb that makes this identification just as obvious: "Whoever is kind to the poor lends to the LORD, and he will reward them for what they have done" (Prov. 19:17).

You mess with them? You're messing with Him. You show mercy to them? You're showing mercy to Him.

When people mock the God of the Bible, this is the God they are mocking: the one who aligns Himself with the last and the weakest; the one who promises to set things right in the end; the one who says the last will be first.

This is His team. His starting lineup consists of the poor and the outcast and the orphan and the alien and the widow. I may be none of those things, but if God identifies with them, I want to identify with them.

This is my team.

And as someone who batted .000 for eight years, it's no wonder this God has great appeal for me.

He has a team, and the roster isn't loaded with superstars. He values that which we do not. He celebrates the uncelebrated.

His team may be in last place now, but make no mistake; it's a promise:

They're going to win.

Acknowledgments

SOME THANKS:

Thank you, coffee, for dilating the blood vessels in my brain and fooling my adrenosine receptors long enough to help me with this book.

And also thank you to this piece of toast right here.

Thank you, Midtown Scholar in Harrisburg, for being an awesome bookstore that lets me sit here way too long.

And thank you, Nicole Courtney, the World's Most Awesome Panera Employee, for teaching me about Williams Syndrome each day while I wrote this. It's fun to swap syndrome stories!

Thank you, custodians and cooks at CURE International hospitals. You are an inspiration. Also, the pastors and nurses and surgeons too! Don't want to forget them. Love you all.

Thank you, SuperDuperStar Editor Meaghan Porter. You are kind to me. And you let me use fragments. When appropriate.

Thank you, misfits who listen to our radio show and

podcast. (We call it an "Oddcast.") As you know, we're not talking to a crowd. We're talking with you. And we're honored, every single day.

Thank you, friends, for putting up with me. I know I'm hard to understand sometimes. Thank you for saying, "That's just Brant; he's odd but we love him," sometimes. Makes me feel good.

———

But mostly, thank you to Carolyn Herron. She's the girl to whom I once blurted out, "I love you." And she's the one who said, "Uh . . . thanks?"

She's my first and only-ever girlfriend. She saw something in me I couldn't see, and now that she's been Carolyn Hansen for a very long time, she still sees something I can't see.

All the while I was writing this book, I wanted to quit. "Who am I to write a book? Who cares what I think?" But she wanted me to read it out loud to her. I did it, embarrassed at the clunkiness of my own sentences. She would listen to every word, occasionally tear up, occasionally laugh—at the right places!—and tell me this book will be helpful to people. And she'd tell me it's good.

You know what? It almost doesn't matter whether it is or not, because Carolyn Hansen, my first and only-ever girlfriend, thinks it is.

Mission accomplished.

A Special Appendix:
A Misfit Roll Call

IF YOU FOUND YOURSELF RELATING TO MANY OF THE ideas in this book, please know it's not just you. It's not even just the two of us.

While writing the book, I described it on social media, and asked once (once!) on social media if anyone else would say, "You know what? That's me, too." So I asked for cosigners. Thousands responded. (We only had room here for a fraction.) Each name represents someone willing to acknowledge their own struggle with long periods of spiritual dryness, doubt, and difficulty relating to church culture, all the while continuing to say, "I still believe."

We're not alone.

Daniel Erickson	Stephanie Neal	John C. Stone
Lee S. King	Landon McAfee	Carl Buff
Karen L. Reyburn	Becky Powers	Brandon Dulaney
Mary Gallagher	Sarah Dunnam	Amy E. Gailey
Arielle Bacon	Julie Pundenberger	Cory Chelf
Emily Ransom	Alicia Root	Bev DeVries
Robin Finney	Andrea Lawson	Brian Sumner

April Hammonds
Melissa Willis
Tim Harold
Lori Seyfried
Lori Shamberger
Scott Stewart
Kiki Lal
Mark Winner
Mike Worrell
Debra Toothaker
DJ Yazell
Melissa Green Marcum
Demetria Elms
Heather Wenner
Kiley Wright
Bri Woigemuth
Megs Neyer
Jennifer L. Lawrence
Stephanie Erickson
Dana Upton
Marty Morningstar
Lisa Joy Stiefken
Tessie Rush
Amanda Drue
Terri Perkins
Soebeck Song
Fayelle Ewuakye
Chri Klotzsche
Heather Haas
Casaundra Tueing
Trish McCaw
Ron Dietrich
Lindsey Adams
Katie Schuette
Carrie Christopher
Bridget Mayo
Samuel Crump

Jodie Greven
Clinton Reed
Suzanne Mexia
Jeremy Cicolino
Maran O'Mera
Annilee Lund
Maryann Landis
Bonnie Thomas
Katie Duffin
Kimberly K. Saunders
Tovah Greenleaf
Andy Reihard
Jon Eccles
Brian Tooley
Brian Neal
Susie Whitinger
Keith Anderson
Kaylee Green
Rachel Green
Kellie Lund
Marie Wignall
Patrick Serban
Dennis Fletcher
Christina Couturier
Zatch Kithoran
Lorrie Runion
Leslie Shults
Kayla Burts
Bryce George
Jennifer Corder
Maranda B. Rice
Melissa Mae Wilson
Diane Broyles
Lonnie Goodin
Bill Scott
Emmy Dupuis
Angie Kelim

Jeff Scott
Kelly Hancock
Billy Ray Duncan
Kimberly L. Marley
Christy Wells-Reece
Amanda Bakaleinikoff
Dan Levengood
Vesta Brown
Matt Rigdon
Shereen Beach
Jess Dycus
Rob Lewis
Ellen Dichaus
Ann Hollensen
Lisa Cuyuch
Benjamin Unander
John Goetz
Lisa K. Dugan
John Reside
Lisa Dell
Jeff Evans
Sandi Carroll
Matt Pelishek
Evelyn Dejesus
Christie Crofford
Brian Siebert
Susan Foley
William Rush
Tanna Fajardo
Lynne L. Harris
Dee McDaniel
Susan K. Carver
Dan Matthews
Dona Howell McPherson
Abbie D. Allan
Ann Faudree
Rachel Fitch

Dave Wonders
Harris Kantner
Kathryn Charlin
Adrienne Martin
Joe Rowsey
Bonnie Bouika
Laura Dunafon
Katrina Giese Dixon
Cruzita Diaz
Megan Albers
Claire Neigenfind
Jen Moser
Laura Tidwell
Lisa Reynolds
Lisa Conway
Patrice Richards-Cooper
Elaine Buenting
Scott Bons
Tiffany L. Hoskinson
Jonathan Meyer
Nicole R. Smith
Gregory Philip Walther
  Holz
Courtney Bellot
Aileen P. Hower
Kia Givens
Annie Steffens
Terra Brady
Michon Noir
Velvet Harper
Jeffry Neill Vanderford
Kim Underwood
Kristi Roth
Makalah Boyer
Dan Young
Michelle Averitt
  Younkman

Greg Hunt
Jocelyn Clarambeau
Faron Dice
Jeanie Gerrick
Richard McClary
Jim Robertson
Zach Groenendal
Jacqueline Pimienta
Rick Curry
J. Castillo
Tamara Arthur
Ron Kopko
William Brent White
Cynthia Espinoza
  Hansen
Josh Lauritch
Paul Tipton
Vicki Kreeger Johnson
Philip G. Worrall
Debbie Mitchell
Navin R. Johnson[*]
Stephanie Ketron Collins
Vicki Petty Gettys
Amberasia Phipps
Victoria Lamb
Joanne Brand
Summer Shepherd
Roger Sigmon
Valerie Clason
Sharaya K. Baker
Karen Paulus
Charles Crutcher
Shayne Howard
Robin Ediger
Ian Chai
Kimberly Townsend
Peggy Clark

Timothy Lowe
Julie Whitmore-Parks
Julie Muytoy
Jay Wright
Linda Dekock
Mary R. Vogt
Linda Hahn
Noemi Jones
Suzy Roberts
Steve Sunshine
Chrissy Fernandez
Karin E. Wirts
Bethany Whitesell
Gray Allen
Tim Payne
Cory Chelf
Paul Anthony Schmitz
Dana McAughty
Jaime Gilleland-Stone
Jessica King
Raven Nichole
Shann Gilman
Caitlin Theroux
Bob Spencer
Cory DeAngelo
Kerrie S. Crowe
Elizabeth Barber
Hannah Branton
Joy Stincic
Scott Herrold
Russell Silverglate
Matt Mundt
Lisa Gilmartin
Judy Diane Rodmaker
Matt Davis
Lisa Moris
Jenn Blankenship

[*] Okay, Brant put this one here.

Eric Loy
MJ Boland
Ruthie Velez
Beth Bacall
Josh Evans
J Bruce Welch
Tracy Stevens
Mike Lee
Liz Lehman Caldieraro
Amy Knight
Kyle Fenton
Linda Mitchell
Mark Stanford
Donna Curcio Binninger
Anna Hagen
Brita Levengood
Lisa Matsuyama
Kara Pitts
Waylon Willoughby
Brooklyn Niemeyer
Rosyline Bethea
Terri Shull-Smith
Elizabeth Moore
Angela R. Huerta
Nancy Kulesza
Christine Dillree
Emily Dell'Amico
Ron Pietrantoni
Michael Edgecomb
Ben Sanders
Nancy S. Cole
Karissa Clayton Jess
Bethany Lemons
Shawn Cochrane
Sarah Hazlewood
Chelsie Geasa
Bethany Clark

Tori Stivers
Leslie Turner
J.D. Mendez
Katie Sexton
Heath Main
Abril Rodriguez
Jenny Jones
Matt Carlock
Kate Voetberg
Susan Irons Crittenden
Wolfman Von
     Hartenberg
Elsea Toscano Cochrane
John W. Turner, Jr.
Kathie Unsell
Kristen Lumsden
Adrienne Henning
Jena Dammeier
BriAnne Johnson
Susan Woolson
Amy Middaugh
Lynn Kirkpatrick
Jeannie Burton
Kim Taylor
Troy Wilson
Karen Ruth
Jonathan Bourque
Bethanne Michelle Parish
TJ Burns
Michael Cote
Ryan Ferrari
Brooke Wilson
Kathie Funke
     Schnakenberg
Sheila Rae Kable
     Mastalski
Gail Rogers

Cassie Eldridge
Gerry Morigerato
Steve Swanson
Chris Tharp
Melissa Dooley
Bob Menge
Monica Sapp
Jennifer Creveling
K. Michelle Cash
Patricia Marshall
Kim Awbrey
Tim Young
Yolanda James
Rita Fox
Caitlynn Bryan
Rhonda H. Erichsen
Paul Condon
Becky Eckheart
Rhonda Basta
Jen Thatcher
Tabitha Kessel
Marilyn Dahl Maloney
Donna Farina-Salustri
Adam Snyder
Amy J. Nelson
Angela Carstens
Brenda Covert
Abbye L. McDonough
Angela Serna
Sarah Hinton
Carl Hamman
Kimberly Graffius
Charlene Heath
Jerri Lyn Larvia
Angela Bumgarner
Amber Edwards
Mark Hahn

Joel Delgado
Kim Zulock
Annie Korf
Shannon Quiles
Natalie Whitney
Traci L. Bryant
Kayla Lykins
Beth Huffman
Lynda Arman
Sandra Cook
Laney McCracken
Cheryl Leiphart
Jacqueline Evans
Mary Kniffen
Jenny Layne
Jennifer Bellomi
Adrienne Scrima
Darin McGee
Kelly Anderson
Hannah Lynn Hand
Matthew Grief
Angela Apodaca
Amanda Fillmore
Danny Guynn
E Barton
Mike Parks
Rhonda Bosgraf Cole
Jill Marie Rthmell
Hannah Chaney
Carrie Rae Wright
Jill Stevenson
Kim Harmon
Danielle Adams
JB Wall
Jennie Heflin
Brenna K. Sullivan
Laurie Russell

Dawn Hopkins
Lauren Porter
Alayna Bryant
Patricia Worth
Darrell Zwanzig
Ann Gupta
Tyler Brian Morgan
Cheryl DuPree
Toni Duddy
Susan Peterson
Jeremy Hall
Ashley Romig
Angela Carper-Venable
Christy Lyn Stephens
Christian Hartley
Thomas Shoffner
Teresa Kalmey
Kainan Jeffers
Tara Ashley
James Poirier
Adria Weger
AmyRenee Sheldon
Jennifer Baird
Wendi Coats
Corri Lutito
Rebecca Rabon
William Atkinson
Jerid Hill
Heather Riggs
Maranda Sedgwick
Res Spears
Melissa Ratliff
Heather Powell
Kristin Hansen
Rachel Ringer
Carissa Parr
Dan Debord

Alicia Pullen
Cynthia George Harrison
Shannon Garris
Andrea Majerle
Sheri Kaetzel
Angelina Dinning
Cody Zander
Jenny M. Madison
Brian Shukwit
Tamara Werner
Cindy Munoz
Deborah Joy Cobb
Nathan Gerber
David Camp
Nicky Lopez
John Frausto
Amanda Wen
Tonya Adams
Pauline Brookhaus
Deborah Wiggin
   Snyder
Rigel Kent Hernaez
Joy Colmery
Isabelle Verhault
Alex Ortiz
Matt Smith
Rachel Flores
Amy Maltrud
Rachel Gilham
Heather Williams
Hannah Callicotte
Tonya R. Franks
Nancy Robinette
Robert Clelland
Julie Hawbaker
Walt McClung
Cheryl Chen

Brenda Sattler
Diane Manning
Dave Mills
Andrew Peeling
Hannah Gilmore
Nancy Hoffman
Mike Madden
Joey Hall
Jessica Hooks
Sue Hewitt
Jennifer Medina
Denise Doucett
Jeannette Stogner
Annie Reed
Emily Riley
Tanya Lyon
Teresa Sparks
Jamie Chhav
Jake Vigesaa
Angie Stevens
Tiff Hill
Beverly Wuellner
Henry M. Ortega
Julie Nightingale
Kiara Kalmey
Meredith Brown
Debby Foster
Cendy Hill
Aubrey Jordan
Veronica Tagle
Heidi Vance
Darlonna Vaughan
Lori Vickers
Aubrey McInturf
Bill Dozier
Thresa Johnson
Lorie Storey

Lindy Lyon
Cas Anderson
Janeen Bair
Karen Shoup
Sami Hency
Karem Duque
Victoria Macaluso
Sarah Dueck
Tracy Thele
Melanie Burkhart
Julia Miller
Charly Miller
Caryle Glowacki
Abby McSheffrey
Amber Stewart
Lisa Troyer
Brian S. Potillo
Candace W. Hovatar
Albert O'Neil
Allison Kofol
Tarah Dalziel
Abby Tolar
Polly Trujillo
Kimberly Guelda
  Stearman
Tanya Miracle
Jeremy John Guelfi
Leslie Lawton Fuller
Mark Cloud
Michael Domizoli
Sarah Spradling
Denise Sharp
Ashley Mallard
Lori Brecheen
Michelle Kaulukukui-
  Palisbo
Jen Sammeroff

Adam McCutcheon
Bethany Watts
Jason C. Joyner
Jessica Hostetter
Laura Elizabeth Brock
Chesney Malabuyo
Stephanie Nolet
Jan Coombs
Kathy Overmyer Goble
Amber Soto
Priscilla Campbell
Kami Whitaker
David Tamayo
Amada A. Ruiz
Julie Burmeister
Josh Mueller
Katie Jernigan
Parker Dawon
Rikki Wade
Kerry M. Adams
Jonathan Lee
Sara McGinness
Missy Grantham
Kelly Larsen
Shelly Gambrell
Melinda Kemp
Marylyn Peklenk
Joshua Miles Hurlburt
Jackeline Sampieri
Seth Kreinbrook
Audrey Coulombe
Jessica Grossman
Lisa Peterson
Vicki L. Seidel
Tiffany Romo
Tina Saavedra
Jo Rush

Beth Warkentin
Jason A.A. Rodriguez
Beka Neeley
Michelle Valdes
Barb Chase
Laura S. Allen
Ellie Rush
Erin Langlois
Sarah Hewitt
Jenn Wallace
Amanda Waller
Carol Ryan
Cindy Ziegler
Holly Steffy
Erin Born
Debbie Lovely
Jennifer Hooper
Thomas Mark Zuniga
Hope Watthanaphand
Rebecca Siemers
Katelyn Frye
Kara Miller
Linda Davis
Andrea Haley
Dan Reihl
Gary Winchester
Melanie Blakeborough
Anna Marie Hall
Amy Enz
Kelli Tipton
Diana Bjarko Fahrenbrck
Jarred Bullock
Beth Knoll
Jonathan Chaney
Norm Bender
Melanie Williams
Jena Pullum

Karen Beth Hansson
Scott Campbell
Kristy Scott
Missy Logsdon
Rob Adams
S. Hoffpauir
Trish Cherry
Angelo Sacks
Christie Landtroop
Kisty Rogers Cox
Quanita Rice
Eugene Byon
Krissy Knoch
Cindy Meyer
Kitty Zeunen
Charmain Zimmerman
  Brackett
Eddie Lockett
Lesa Brackbill
Ann Marie Hemstreet
Kurt Eilander
Dawn Kneller
Mike Thompson
Doug Schaefer
Lee Ann Hohenstein
Frank Williams
Daniel Akers
Christine Cornell
  Hawkins
Kelie Taylor
Teresa House
Tamber Craig
Christa Morris
Michelle Marren
Amy L. Florence
Oneida McMann
Kedrin Bell

Robert Durough
Stazie Church
Gabriella Epinoza
Ellen J. Tung
Rachael Davis
Tiena Bruner
Beth McConn
Venessa Oldham
Christi Estanovich
Joy Noel Barber
Carla Williamson
Erin Brown
Kelsey Elizabeth
  Cooper
Rebecca Hanneman
Lori Vickers
Judy Gantzer
Bethany Bidwell
Deborah Snedecor
Morgan Jobe
Jen Medsker
Kayla Lykins
Karrie McLeod
Jackie Cartwright
Paula Esser
Andy Alfonso
Danielle Freeman
Julie Starliper
Ashley Fontenot
Eryn Davis
Dr. Brent Johnson
Christine Robinson
April Jolene Lehman
Lisa Chen
Debra Lynne Kam
Vicky Huber
Alicia Joy Kessener

Eric James Copeland

Debbie Ann Dominquez

Bethany Watts

Marilyn Hannam Pinney

Kris Broyles

Vicki Lynn Bray

Melissa A. Hall

Jennifer King Eason

Tammy Westbrook

Naomi Kemp

Diana Kennedy

Cindy Kriegel

Vickie Mertz

Cynthia Greise Gladden

Kathy Haikey

Amanda DeWilde

April Ward

Terese Van Liew

Kelly Causie Figh

Sarah Spradling

Amber Owens

Tonya Mikeworth

Shelby O'Lammy and
the Isle of Misfits
Ranch

Angelica S. Diaz

Janis Flynn

Jordon Speckhardt

Grant Kelly

Janice Ryman

Jeff Gregory

Kelly Gomer

Robyn Fortenberry

Deb Caparoon

Notes

Foreword

1. Brant Hansen, "'Mr. Spock Goes to Church': How One Christian Copes with Asperger's Syndrome," *CNN Belief Blog*, October 19, 2013, http://religion.blogs.cnn.com/2013/10/19/mr -spock-goes-to-church-how-one-christian-copes-with-aspergers -syndrome/.

Chapter 2: Together, yet Apart

1. Hayyim Schauss, "Ancient Jewish Marriage," *My Jewish Learning*, accessed April 28, 2017, http://www.myjewishlearning.com/article /ancient-jewish-marriage/.
2. Maurice Lamm, "The Jewish Marriage Ceremony," Chabad.org, accessed April 29, 2017, http://www.chabad.org/library/article _cdo/aid/465162/jewish/The-Jewish-Marriage-Ceremony.htm.
3. Sidney L. Markowitz, *What You Should Know About Jewish History, Ethics, and Culture* (Hoboken, NJ: Citadel Press, 1982), 172.

Chapter 3: Blessed Are My Fellow People on the Autism Spectrum (and Those Who Can Relate to Us)

1. Tania Lombrozo, "Do You Suffer from Illusions of Moral Superiority?," npr.org, January 23, 2017, http://www.npr.org /sections/13.7/2017/01/23/511164613/do-you-suffer-from -illusions-of-moral-superiority.

Chapter 5: Blessed Are the Unfeeling Faithful

1. Brian Kolodiejchuk, *Mother Teresa: Come Be My Light; The Private Writings of the Saint of Calcutta* (New York: Doubleday, 2009), 288.
2. Christopher Hitchens, *The Missionary Position* (Toronto: McClelland & Stewart, 2012).
3. Gerald May, *The Dark Night of the Soul: A Psychiatrist Explores the Connection Between Darkness and Spiritual Growth* (San Francisco: HarperSanFrancisco, 2005), 92–93.
4. Adam McHugh, *Introverts in the Church: Finding Our Place in an Extroverted Culture* (Downers Grove, IL: IVP Books, 2009), 75.
5. T. M. Luhrmann, "My Take: If You Hear God Speak Audibly, You (Usually) Aren't Crazy," *CNN Belief Blog*, December 29, 2012, http://religion.blogs.cnn.com/2012/12/29/my-take-if-you-hear-god-speak-audibly-you-usually-arent-crazy/.
6. David Van Biema, "Mother Teresa's Crisis of Faith," TIME.com, August 23, 2007, http://time.com/4126238/mother-teresas-crisis-of-faith/.
7. Wesley Hill, *Washed and Waiting* (Grand Rapids, MI: Zondervan, 2010), 71.

Chapter 6: Blessed Are the Unfeeling Faithful, Part 2: Real "Fruit"

1. Eugene Peterson, *A Long Obedience in the Same Direction* (Downers Grove, IL: InterVarsity Press, 2000), 29.

Chapter 7: Blessed Are the Introverted Evangelical Failures

1. Francis Chan, "Chan: The Biggest Myth in the Church Today on Evangelism," ChurchLeaders.com, December 29, 2013, http://churchleaders.com/outreach-missions/outreach-missions-articles/163926-chan-biggest-myth-church-today-evangelism.html.
2. Alan Kreider, "Worship and Evangelism in Pre-Christendom: The Laing Lecture, 1994," BiblicalStudies.org.uk, accessed

April 29, 2017, https://biblicalstudies.org.uk/pdf/vox/vol24
/worship_kreider.pdf.

3. Ibid.

Chapter 8: Blessed Are the People Who Can't Pray Worth a Darn

1. Michael Lipka, "5 Facts About Prayer," Pew Research, May 4, 2016, http://www.pewresearch.org/fact-tank/2016/05/04/5 -facts-about-prayer/.

Chapter 9: Blessed Are the People Who Just Read That Last Chapter but Still Have Some Questions

1. C. S. Lewis, *Essential C. S. Lewis* (New York: Touchstone, 1996), 381.

Chapter 10: Blessed Are the Wounded

1. Brant Hansen, *Unoffendable* (Nashville: Thomas Nelson, 2015).

2. Henri Nouwen, "July 8," in *Bread for the Journey* (New York: HarperCollins, 1996), Kindle location 2474.

Chapter 11: Blessed Are Those Who Don't Have Amazing Spiritual Stories

1. "Seinfeld—To Be Continued," YouTube video, 0:53, from a *Seinfeld* episode televised in 1992 by Castle Rock Entertainment and Sony Pictures Television, posted by "vhsclassic90s," August 1, 2014, https://www.youtube.com/watch?v=YPOh_xtnVbc.

Chapter 12: Blessed Are the Impostors

1. Carl Richards, "Learning to Deal with the Impostor Syndrome," NYTimes.com, October 26, 2015, http://www.nytimes.com /2015/10/26/your-money/learning-to-deal-with-the-impostor -syndrome.html.

Chapter 14: Blessed Are the Perpetual Strugglers

1. J. R. R. Tolkien, *The Lord of the Rings: Fellowship of the Ring* (New York, Houghton Mifflin, 1954), 274.
2. Richard Foster, *Prayer: Finding the Heart's True Home* (San Francisco: HarperCollins, 2002), 67.
3. McHugh, *Introverts in the Church*, 59.

Chapter 15: Blessed Are the People Who Do Church Anyway

1. C. S. Lewis, *The Four Loves* (New York: Harcourt Brace, 1960), 61.
2. N. T. Wright, *Jesus and the Victory of God* (London: SPCK Publishing, 1996), 297.
3. Ibid., 296.
4. Darryl Tippens, "Loneliness and Community: An Interview with Henri Nouwen," Wineskins.org, March–August 1994, accessed April 30, 2017, http://archives.wineskins.org/article/loneliness-and-community-an-interview-with-henri-nouwen-mar-aug-1994/.
5. Gilbert K. Chesterton, *What's Wrong with the World* (New York: Dodd, Mead and Company, 1912), 67–68.

Chapter 16: Blessed Are the Melancholy and the Depressed

1. Gilbert K. Chesterton, *Orthodoxy* (New York: John Lane Company, 1909), 22.

Chapter 17: Blessed Are Those Who Don't Take Themselves So Seriously

1. Peterson, *A Long Obedience in the Same Direction*, 54.
2. Steven Curtis Chapman, "Fingerprints of God," on *Speechless*, Sparrow Records, 1999.
3. Connie Robertson, ed., *Dictionary of Quotations*, 3rd ed. (Hertfordshire, UK: Wordsworth, 1998), 31.

4. C. S. Lewis, *Letters to Malcolm: Chiefly on Prayer* (San Diego: Harvest, 1964), 93.

5. Gilbert K. Chesterton, *Heretics* (1905; repr., Nashville: Sam Torode Book Arts, n.d.), 54.

6. Roy Rosenbaum, "An Interview with Bob Dylan," cited in Southern Cross Review, accessed April 30, 2017, http://www.southerncrossreview.org/41/dylan.htm.

Chapter 18: Blessed Are the Skeptics and Those Who Don't Know Where Else to Go

1. Richard Dawkins, *River Out of Eden: A Darwinian View of Life* (New York: Basic Books, 1995), 133.

2. Larry Taunton, "Richard Dawkins: The Atheist Evangelist," Larry Alex Taunton (website), April 13, 2017, http://larryalextaunton.com/articles/richard-dawkins-the-atheist-evangelist/.

3. Sam Harris, *Letter to a Christian Nation* (New York: Knopf, 2006), 25.

4. Graham Templeton, "Neil deGrasse Tyson Says It's 'Very Likely' the Universe Is a Simulation," ExtremeTech, April 22, 2016, https://www.extremetech.com/extreme/227126-neil-degrasse-tyson-says-its-very-likely-the-universe-is-a-simulation.

5. Stephane Courtois, *The Black Book of Communism: Crimes, Terror, Repression* (Cambridge, MS: Harvard University Press, 1996), 92–97, 116–21.

6. Jonathan Haidt, *The Happiness Hypothesis: Finding Modern Truth in Ancient Wisdom* (New York, Basic Books, 2006), 89.

7. "Heroin Deaths in the US Surpass Gun Homicides," *Lake Tahoe News*, December 11, 2016, http://www.laketahoenews.net/2016/12/heroin-deaths-u-s-surpass-gun-homicides/.

8. Ross Douthat, "All the Lonely People," NYTimes.com, May 28, 2013, http://www.nytimes.com/2013/05/19/opinion/sunday/douthat-loneliness-and-suicide.html.

9. May, *The Dark Night of the Soul*, 65–66.

10. C. S. Lewis, *The Weight of Glory* (New York: HarperCollins, 1949), 31.

Chapter 19: Blessed Are the Unnoticed
1. Taunton, "Richard Dawkins."

Chapter 20: Blessed Are the Lonely
1. Angelina Jolie, "Anne Hathaway," *Interview*, October 1, 2005, http://www.interviewmagazine.com/film/anne-hathaway/#_.
2. Katie Hafner, "Researchers Confront an Epidemic of Loneliness," NYTimes.com, September 5, 2016, http://www.nytimes.com /2016/09/06/health/lonliness-aging-health-effects.html.
3. Brant Hansen, "Yearning for the Undeniable God," branthansen.com, July 28, 2014, http://branthansen.com /2014/07/28/yearning-for-the-undeniable-god/.
4. Ibid.

Chapter 21: Blessed Are the Misfit Royalty
1. James C. McKinley Jr., "Sports Psychology; It Isn't Just a Game: Clues to Avid Rooting," NYTimes.com, August 11, 2000, http://www.nytimes.com/2000/08/11/sports/sports -psychology-it-isn-t-just-a-game-clues-to-avid-rooting.html.

About the Author

BRANT HANSEN IS A SYNDICATED RADIO HOST heard nationwide on more than two hundred stations and on the popular *Brant and Sherri Oddcast* podcast.

His writing has been featured online by CNN, the *Washington Post*, *Relevant Magazine*, and *US News and World Report*.

He also speaks across the country about his faith, his life as an "Aspie" (he was diagnosed with an Autism Spectrum Disorder), and his work with CURE International, a remarkable global network of hospitals treating children with correctible disabilities. (Find out more at CURE.org.)

Follow Brant on Twitter and Instagram at @branthansen, "Brant Hansen Page" on Facebook, or at Branthansen.com.